# More Praise for *Mom-in-Chief*

"Jamie Woolf, twenty-year veteran in leadership training, has taken her corporate coaching skills into the kitchen and finally taught us that it's not about child development, it's about mom development. Not a bunch of theories, just clear-cut leadership skills that you take out of your tool box when needed. Bedside reading for every conscientious mother—or father."

—Alexia Nye Jackson,
founder and CEO of MOTHER: THE JOB

"I was *very* impressed by the whole premise of *Mom-in-Chief*. That's a good sign, since I am the least corporate person on the planet, and all leadership jargon gives me the hives. But Jamie Woolf makes it sound reasonable, rational, and very helpful. I feel like I'll be a better mom already."

—Regan McMahon, author, *Revolution in the Bleachers:
How Parents Can Take Back Family Life
in a World Gone Crazy Over Youth Sports*

"I love that parents can translate their leadership skills to parenting *without* making their homes look more like their workplaces. *Mom-in-Chief* clearly shows parents that they already have the skills they need to parent in a way that is more fun, more effective, and more rewarding. Say good-bye to exhausting end-of-the-day meltdowns and frustrating battles with food and homework: being a mom doesn't have to be so hard."

—Christine Carter, PhD; executive director,
Greater Good Science Center at the University of California–
Berkeley; and author of the blog *Half Full:
Science for Raising Happy Kids*

# Mom
## -in-
# Chief

# Mom

## -in-
## Chief

## How Wisdom *from the* Workplace Can Save Your Family *from* Chaos

### Jamie Woolf

FOREWORD BY CAROL EVANS

A *WORKING MOTHER* MAGAZINE BOOK

JOSSEY-BASS
A Wiley Imprint
www.josseybass.com

Published by Jossey-Bass
A Wiley Imprint
989 Market Street, San Francisco, CA 94103-1741—www.josseybass.com

Jossey-Bass books and products are available through most bookstores. To contact
Jossey-Bass directly call our Customer Care Department within the U.S. at 800-956-
7739, outside the U.S. at 317-572-3986, or fax 317-572-4002.

Jossey-Bass also publishes its books in a variety of electronic formats. Some content
that appears in print may not be available in electronic books.

**Library of Congress Cataloging-in-Publication Data**

Woolf, Jamie, date.
    Mom-in-chief : how wisdom from the workplace can save your family from
chaos / Jamie Woolf ; foreword by Carol Evans. — 1st ed.
        p.   cm.
    Includes bibliographical references and index.
    ISBN 978-0-470-38131-1 (cloth)
        1.  Parenting.   2. Family.   3. Leadership.   4. Work and family.   I. Title.
HQ755.8.W675 2009
646.7'8—dc22

                                                                            2008041899

Printed in the United States of America
FIRST EDITION
HB Printing    10 9 8 7 6 5 4 3 2 1

# CONTENTS

# FOREWORD

Jamie Woolf came to me last year with a brilliant idea. She wanted to write a book about how to take the leadership skills that we develop at work back into the home to make our families, our marriages, and our work-life balance more manageable—and more successful. I was thrilled with her concept. We work so hard to build our management and leadership skills in our careers, but we often feel like blithering idiots when faced with a child who won't cooperate, a husband who doesn't pay attention, and a household that seems ready to collapse under the weight of our anxiety about chores. "Why can't I be as smart at home as I am at work?" I have often found myself wondering.

Indeed, why?

Jamie Woolf has written *Mom-in-Chief* to give us a lifetime's worth of ideas, tips, and solutions for how to find our strength at home by transferring our skills from career to family. She tells us, in rich stories and easy activities, how to leap forward in our personal satisfaction with our work-life balance.

I first met Jamie when I was looking for an expert to help me turn my own book, *This Is How We Do It*, into a workshop for moms and dads. Jamie's enthusiasm was contagious. She had been working as an executive coach for moms and dads for years, and had taught parenting skills and work-life balance to thousands of people at companies all across the country.

But most important, she was and of course still is in the midst of raising two daughters herself, so she speaks from a deeply personal side about the frustrations, exhaustion, and confusion that parenting creates—and that no one can really understand unless he or she is doing it! Jamie has fought hard to create a life that gives her the balance she wants.

But the reason I was so excited about her book is that Jamie has a big-picture idea. She knows that it is the long view of parenting, of careers, and of relationships that gives us the best chance of creating change in our own lives. She knows that quick-fix gimmicks sound good but don't pay off. So she gives us a whole series of easy, step-by-step methods to bring the long view into focus and train ourselves for a better life.

Carol Evans
CEO, Working Mother Media

For Anna and Leah
For Marjory Woolf, my Mom-in-Chief

# ACKNOWLEDGMENTS

How many transformational leaders does it take to write a book? So many that I fear it's inevitable that I will leave out people who deserve my thanks. Writing this book has put me on the receiving end of the most extraordinary leaders. First, Joe Di Prisco. Without his belief in me, this book would remain an unfulfilled dream. Thanks to Joe also for connecting me to our beloved literary agent, Liz Trupin-Pulli. Liz believed in me from the get-go, through the rejections and at every critical junction along the way. Eternal thanks to Diane Delsignore for the introduction to Joe and, more important, for her friendship. My gratitude goes to Jim Kouzes, whose enthusiasm about the power of transformational leadership and brilliant book *The Leadership Challenge* inspired a lifelong passion in me. I thank him too for the encouragement and astute advice about writing a book and getting published.

Special thanks to Alan Rinzler, my editor at Jossey-Bass, who enthusiastically supported my idea from the start. Alan kept me on what seemed like an impossibly ambitious schedule with just the right amount of pushing and trusting. And enormous gratitude to my editor and friend Laura Fraser. (Laura, how many times can I write thank you thank you thank you in one sentence? You were never more than an e-mail away, continually sending me your words of encouragement, transforming paragraphs of wordswordswords and making them snap and sparkle.) And thanks to all my writing friends and unrelenting supporters: Katherine Ozment, for believing in the worth of my book proposal even when it was a bloody mess; Erica Etelson; Beverly Berning; Ilana Debare; Robin Gerber; Cecelia Cancellaro; Julie Harris; Dianne Jacob; Amy Schoenblum; Jamie Traeger-Muney; Sharon Weinberg; and David Schweizer. And a gigantic thank you to Regan McMahon, whose gifted writing and parenting acumen were invaluable. A whopping thanks to Trudi Roth, who believed in my idea when it was still fuzzy and kept me going with her unflagging support and sense of humor. And special thanks to Jhay Greene for his wisdom, encouragement, hair therapy, and generous networking. Thank you to Ruth Fallenbaum for being my ally no matter what. Her ability to cut through the confusion never ceases to amaze me.

Thanks to the team at Jossey-Bass/Wiley—Michele Jones for her amazingly thorough and precise copyediting, Nana Twumasi, Carol Hartland, Michael Onorato, Jennifer Wenzel, and Carrie Wright.

I want to thank the team at *Working Mother* magazine, Suzanne Riss, Tammy Palazzo, Barbara Turvett, Barbara Rosenthal, Teresa Palagano, and especially Carol Evans, whose enthusiasm and encouragement are more uplifting than I can express in mere words.

Special thanks go to my clients, who inspire me and teach me humbling lessons about how hard it is to be a great leader, and to the generosity and wisdom of all the parents, children, and teachers who shared their stories with awe-inspiring honesty and insight. To Valerie Weller; Jane Griswold; Sam Schuchat; Steve Leonoudakis; Debbie Bonzell; Elaine Fukuhara Schilling; Dana Zed; Laura Garcia-Moreno; Lynn Lazurus; Heather Swallow; Molly Rosen; Vanessa Van Petten; Tami Benau; Lee Hsu; Julie Reinganum; Nancy Ortberg; Christine Carter; Lorne, Elissa, and Michelle Buchman; Marc and Amy Vachon; John Tannen; Gwen Hornig; Chris Hiroshima; Mary Olivella; Phyllis

Hoffman; Diana Verdugo; Beth Goldberg; Lynn Bravewomon; Barbara Leslie; and many others: I hope I did your stories justice.

Thank you to Rabbi Steven Chester for providing the best example of leadership I know.

Big appreciation goes to Dr. Barbara Waterman for her wisdom, savvy edits, and generous counsel. And thanks to Dr. Susan Greene for sharing so clearly her deep experience with children. Kudos to Henry Koltys for a close reading and his willingness to share his savoir faire after one lunch.

I will be forever grateful to Lian Dolan for opening doors, for her savvy advice, and for sharing her own story so honestly. She's the best sister-in-law an only child could hope for.

Thanks to my personal support team, starting with my mom, Marjory Woolf, whose love and support make me feel like the best daughter and mother on the planet even when I'm cranky and impatient. She is the model I carry with me when I'm at my best with Anna and Leah. I know she's completely biased, but her pride lifts me up anyway. And to Mack Sturgis, we all miss you. Your laughter, integrity, and love are felt every day.

A gigantic thanks to David Green, who picked me up after rejections, bore the brunt of my highs and lows, and guided me through hoops and over hurdles. His astute insights improved the book by leaps and bounds. I can't thank him enough for his friendship and indefatigable support, and for providing me with a room of my own.

Everyone deserves a friend like Erika Tunick. She is a saint even if she denies it. I am deeply grateful for Alice Fishman, my lifelong devoted friend, keen reader, and Excel spreadsheet wiz. A huge thanks to my dear friend Heidi Rosenfelder, who organized and sat through more of my workshops than anyone should have to, but, because she's Heidi, did so with unsurpassed grace. And thank you to Denise Green for reading my proposal and giving me the keen guidance of a true writer. Thanks to Rona Bar Din for reading chapters way before they were ripe and still giving me enthusiastic encouragement. Thank you to Ann and Barney Mizel for all the heartfelt support and networking. Thank you to my many friends who rallied, cheered, and understood when I neglected them in order to get this book finished.

I owe eternal thanks to my husband, Burke Treidler, for putting up with my book-writing mood swings and late-night obsessions; for reading chapters even when the soccer championships were on TV; for giving me honest feedback along with the requisite smiley faces to balance the red-pen markup; for doing more than his share of the grocery shopping, cooking, and tax and tech support; and most of all, for his unconditional love. Without you, Burke, this book would not exist.

And finally to my amazing daughters, Anna and Leah. Thanks for patiently putting up with me and cheering me on during my writing months. You are my heart, my life. You inspire me to be a better person every day.

# Mom

## -in-
## Chief

# Introduction

It has been said that the hardest job in the world is raising a child, but the people who say this have probably never worked in a comb factory or captured pirates on the high seas.
—Lemony Snicket

It's 4:30 in the afternoon, and I've been in the office since 6:30 this morning. I grab the chic messenger bag I bought myself when I was promoted to manager, and pretend I'm invisible as I dash down the hallway, avoiding eye contact with anyone who might impede my early escape. I run down the garage stairs and into my car, where I scribble on the yellow pad in the passenger's seat, writing a quick to-do list for tomorrow's day at the office while my mind is still speeding with the events of the day, trying to wrap it all up and clear my head of work.

The past ten hours have been challenging, but the day ended well. I led a productive meeting. My staff came up with some pretty exciting strategies to deal with proposed budget cuts. I am exhausted but exhilarated. Twenty minutes later, my headlights cut through thick fog as I exit the freeway, nearing home.

But as I turn right on to my street, my sense of the day's accomplishments starts to fade. I begin to feel mixed emotions—joy at the thought of seeing my daughter and dread at what the evening before us might bring.

# THE WAR ON THE HOME FRONT

Before I'm out of the car, Anna, three years old, runs into the garage and squeals, "Mommy's home!" I get a delicious hug, and she pulls me upstairs as Chang Rong, our caregiver, gives me her daily report: Anna ate pistachio nuts, napped for twenty minutes, played with her alphabet puzzle, and pooped. Chang Rong leaves. She has her own family to take care of too.

I look through the mail while Anna holds the pipe cleaner kitty she made at preschool in front of my eyes. As she's making kitty sound effects, it occurs to her that she's dying of starvation. We run downstairs together in a flash, and suddenly I'm bustling around the kitchen, setting water to boil, pouring juice and toasting an English muffin for her quick snack while we're waiting, and consoling her that yes, of course her pipe cleaner contraption looks exactly like a kitty and no, I don't think it looks more like a dog.

The phone rings. It's my husband saying he can't come home early tomorrow and watch Anna while our nanny is out of town. What am I going to do? There's a directors' meeting I can't miss in the afternoon, as I'm the one leading it.

There's a crash as Anna knocks over the stool she's perched on to reach the table. Her juice glass has shattered, and now she's crying, having bumped her head on the sticky orange floor.

I'm running out of patience (has it been only thirty minutes since I got home?), and my husband, Burke, won't be back for another two hours. I fix dinner at breakneck speed, spurred on by my daughter's whining. I spoon out the undercooked pasta, add a little tomato sauce from a jar, and serve up a plate of spaghetti for her. Voila.

"I don't feel like spaghetti," my daughter whimpers tragically. "I wanted macaroni and cheese."

I'm seething. Why can't I think of an effective strategy to deal with my lovable kid's mood swings? After all, I deal with impetuous adults at work all day long. But somehow all those workplace skills go out the window when Anna starts her act as the resident drama queen, mucous from her nose mixing with the hot tears pouring down her cheeks, and a bit of blood on her knee to boot. Next thing I know, I'm hollering, sweeping her up and running back upstairs to get her special Dora the Explorer Band-Aids, angry at myself and my child.

My in-control professional self has leaked away nearly completely by the time my husband arrives. Burke isn't thrilled to see that there's no food on the table. He is able to calm Anna down, but is not much help making or cleaning up dinner for the three of us, so by 8 PM, I'm wasted, burned out, depressed, and ready for bed. How can I feel so effective at work and so diminished at home?

This was not, needless to say, the first time something like this had happened. After managing a team of professionals charged with delivering in-house staff and leadership training programs to over nine thousand employees, I found myself, once again, faced with an unhappy child, a chaotic household, and not an ounce of patience to spare. On top of my impatience, I feel guilt—I'm fortunate to have a good job, a two-parent household, and a healthy three-year-old (we hadn't yet had our second daughter, Leah). I wrestle with a confusing mixture of gratitude and exhaustion.

## AN "AHA" MOMENT

The next day, I took a midmorning break alone, just for myself, and went for a walk around the downtown center where our office was located in a metal and glass industrial high-rise.

I had to do something about this. Just as I was arriving where I'd wanted to be after all those years of school and of working my way up the organizational hierarchy, getting married, and becoming a mother, my life was becoming unmanageable and things were falling apart. I had no idea what the problems of "having it all" would be, how trying to juggle work and home was leading to stress and strain for the people I loved the most.

It was surprising how tired and exhausted I felt on this walk after only thirty minutes or so. Must be the chronic sleep deprivation, I said to myself, stumbling back into my office and closing the door so that no one would disturb me. I sat down at my computer and stared at it, unable to get back into work mode.

But then . . . with visions of Anna's face screwed up with petulance, just as I was about to melt into a heap of frustration, something clicked.

I'm a good manager, I said to myself. I've proven myself in the workplace and have leadership skills honed in competitive corporate America as well as in the ivory towers of universities. At work, I know how to build strong relationships, inspire enthusiasm, and quell conflicts. I can do this. So why can't I use those same battle-tested leadership tools when I get home? Bringing leadership skills to parenting not only made perfect sense but also suddenly seemed like a survival strategy. At that moment I started working on a whole new plan of action.

This "Aha" moment gave me newfound energy to figure out how to translate the best of my workplace leadership skills to my role as a mom. It was time to design a leadership program for parents based on my twenty years of experience consulting to business managers and executives.

## TRANSFERRING SKILLS FROM WORK TO HOME

The results of using leadership techniques at home were impressive from the very beginning, and gave me a kind of satisfaction I hadn't fully experienced before as a mother. As I developed the means of transferring these skills from work to home, I began to speak in workplaces; for professional organizations, schools, parenting groups, churches and temples; and at conferences hosted by *Working Mother* magazine. As I met more and more women like me at these events—moms who were effective at work, frustrated at home—I found a universal craving for the sense of fullness of self that the job of being a mother had denied them.

I decided I wanted to help moms discover that when they claimed their roles as leaders at home, they were more effective with their children and felt better about themselves, and the whole family experienced more success and joy. That new awareness resonated with the working mothers I met all across the country.

I wondered why so many women, myself included, leave their leadership skills at the front door when they arrive home. Is it because, as a mom, you can't fire or transfer your children when they misbehave, and you can't give your children a bonus or a promotion to motivate them to clean their room? No. That wasn't it. At the university where I had once worked, we barely had merit increases each year. And as for firing, I learned, at least in my current public sector setting, that you'd have to embezzle a lot of money or trash your neighbor's cubicle to get fired from the workplace these days. Besides, the best leaders, in my experience, didn't rely on a carrot-and-stick approach.

Is it, as my friend Leslie suggested, that the job of mom includes so much drudgery? I don't think so. A good chunk of my workday was spent on bureaucratic paperwork that made wiping my daughter's nose pretty darn appealing.

Was it the exhaustion of working full-tilt all day only to go home and pull a second shift? That's closer to the mark—along with the fact that we often don't get the personal rewards, remuneration, promotions, or support at home that we get at work. There is still precious little status associated with mother's work, and although I wish the world were different, I don't see that changing anytime soon.

Even the feminist Betty Friedan, in *The Feminine Mystique*, said of mothers, "the work they do does not require adult capabilities; it is endless, monotonous, unrewarding." This common view undercuts the leadership work of parenting. The stigma remains that the job of mother is not real work.

No wonder we come home and feel diminished.

In a culture that doesn't acknowledge the high-level skills required for the job of mothering, we have to generate our own sense of value. As my friend Marina, forty-eight, mother of two, says, "In my house I'm the President of Human Potential." Just approaching motherhood as a leadership job can start you thinking in a new way that makes going home to your kids feel less like a grind and more like an exciting challenge.

Few people realize at first that work and parenting inform each other. The best-selling parenting book *What to Expect When You're Expecting* claims that your career-oriented self dies with your baby's birth. But that's just not true for the working mothers I have spoken to. Our career-oriented self may be eclipsed for a while, but it comes back when we're ready. The professional and parenting aspects of our identities are mutually enhancing. Our challenge as working moms is to bring what we learn from our work to our home experiences so that we're left less fragmented and more effective in both worlds.

## THE SIMILARITIES BETWEEN BUSINESSES AND FAMILIES

I have grown more and more convinced that businesses and families aren't all that different. In my own work, I'm excited not by the daily tasks but by the human psychology behind them— staying focused on the big picture, motivating people to do work that is not always interesting, connecting with them, developing their skills, and helping staff discover their true talents. That is the stuff of great leadership—and it is no different than the sophisticated range of skills required for the job of mother. In fact, the most successful leaders and parents today have the same set of strategies, chief among them

1. Setting clear goals
2. Cultivating self-awareness
3. Managing conflict
4. Fostering a healthy culture

5. Managing crises
6. Navigating difficult relationships
7. Balancing priorities

As more women delay parenting until after they build careers, it's natural that they will bring their professional skills to the parenting role. And it's a relief for these moms to use those well-honed leadership tools at home. The mothers I've worked with found that using leadership techniques at home helped them feel less like overburdened servants and more like competent, effective family leaders. Being a Mom-in-Chief was a significant and deserved promotion.

## WHAT IS EFFECTIVE LEADERSHIP?

James MacGregor Burns, a pioneer in the study of leadership, coined the term *transformational leader* to describe the leader who guides others to reach their highest aspirations. What transformational leaders do closely corresponds with what the best parents do. The transformational leader strives to provide the proper conditions for others to grow and be creative, and consults with others when possible so that they have a voice in decisions that affect them. Burns referred to parenting as "the initial act of leadership," expanding the notion of leadership beyond the walls of presidential mansions and corporate suites. Leadership transcends formal titles. Leaders are found at all levels within organizations, just as leadership is found in the home.

Women, research shows, are more likely to demonstrate transformational leadership in the workplace than men, helping employees develop their skills and soliciting cooperation rather than exercising power over people. This makes mothers especially well equipped for leadership—their transformational leadership skills are at the very core of good parenting.

## THE CRISIS IN FAMILY LEADERSHIP

I believe there is a leadership crisis in many families today. Parenting style has swung from an older generation's command-and-control tactics, exercised in families where ideally the child is seen and not heard, to the new generation's abnegation of parental leadership in the face of the all-important and all-demanding child. Many parents raised on Question Authority slogans struggle to accept the role of leader, equating leadership with oppression. The aversion to leadership plays out in a number of ways: we see helicopter moms, hovering over the child's every move; over-the-top soccer moms sacrificing their leisure time not only to drive children to and from games but also to attend each game as well; and mothers who try to be their child's best friend, granting him equal say-so in all matters. Parents' shirking their leadership responsibilities leaves children without the guardrails that set boundaries for unacceptable behavior and create safety barriers for unrestrained impulses.

As one mother asked me during one of my trainings, "How can this three-foot person have so much power over me?" Something's not working when otherwise capable adults feel inept when it comes to managing their child—but it's something families can fix.

We've all suffered from poorly run workplaces and bosses who have made our lives miserable. We may have felt victimized by ineffective leadership in our schools, communities, businesses, and government.

Poorly run families risk the same kind of brokenness: continual power struggles with no one taking responsibility. Inevitably, when a parent reneges on her leadership role, intolerable behavior ensues, and, in desperation, the parent resorts to an authority eruption (exactly the kind of power the parent was defending against in the first place), then often feels guilty. To combat the guilt, the parent bends over backwards to accommodate the child, and the cycle continues. It's a vicious circle.

With transformational leadership, you assume your rightful position as boss, without the aggressive power the Question Authority generation guards against. What we've learned from great leadership and healthy workplaces can be applied to parenting. This book is about taking the best of leadership home, where it matters most.

## LEADERSHIP SKILLS YOU CAN BRING HOME FROM WORK

Stacks of leadership books have been written, each with a slightly different slant on what makes a good leader. Which leadership skills are especially useful in running a family? What skills do working mothers learn in their professional lives that help them raise healthy, happy children? I have seen great acts of leadership at all organizational levels, in all sorts of workplaces. I've witnessed skillful leadership in the aisles of grocery stores and at kitchen tables. From my experience consulting with and coaching hundreds of leaders across a diversity of industries, I have gleaned five skill sets that are most important for Mom-in-Chief leadership:

1. Motivate
2. Focus on the big picture
3. Empower
4. Connect
5. Set an example

This book will help you set in motion each of these areas of expertise with your family.

### Motivate

The most effective business leaders inspire people to step up and take responsibility and to perform at a high level even without bonuses and other perks.

For instance, Diana Verdugo stepped in to take over a flailing work-study department at her college. People were cynical—clocking out not a minute past five, unenthusiastic, and looking for other jobs. By listening to people, valuing their input, and raising expectations, Diana tapped into their talents and turned the department around.

At home, she recognized that the same skills worked with her daughter, Lauryn. She remembers the delicate balancing act that was required to keep her daughter, now a successful musician and doctoral candidate in ethnomusicology, motivated to continue her piano studies. Diana kept expectations high but not so high that she discouraged her daughter. She knew that Lauryn needed to be intrinsically motivated, that piano had to be enjoyable and not made into a boring chore, and that she could unwittingly de-motivate her daughter if she imposed her will. Today Lauryn thanks her mom for encouraging her passions when she was young.

### Focus on the Big Picture

The big picture, objectives, goals, visions, and missions are all fodder for "Dilbert" cartoons, but the fact remains: leaders keep their eye on the long view, looking beyond the task at hand to the greater purpose. They understand that their actions today can have a long-term effect.

When her colleagues engage in petty conflicts, Karen Coyne, a social worker at a hospital, prompts them to remember their larger objectives. "Without being holier-than-thou, I say we're forgetting about why we're here in the first place, to get people back to health." At the very least, this mentality helps her remain enthusiastic and avoid burnout.

Like many mothers, Karen sometimes feels overwhelmed by the relentless demands of two young children at home, losing sight of the bigger picture as she breaks up sibling quarrels, manages temper tantrums, and changes the diapers. As at work, she tries to focus on her objectives when she's on the brink of throwing up her hands. "I just couldn't take it anymore—the whining, the lost jackets, the homework battles," she says. "But I take a breath, maybe even go into my room and close the door, and remember that my objective is to raise responsible human beings." This helps her keep her cool and find creative ways to teach her children to assume responsibility.

## Empower

Stella, a school administrator, seeks out ways to increase the autonomy of her direct reports. Having grown up with three older brothers, she found that relinquishing hard-won control didn't come naturally. But she saw what happened when she restricted the independence of the people with whom she worked, and made decisions without engaging them. She sets clear guidelines and enforces reasonable rules, but she realizes that when she trusts people, they rise to her expectations. When problems arise, she conducts meetings, and trusts that if she doesn't step in, people will come up with creative solutions. Her approach inspires confidence and fosters ownership in the solution. She gives people the skills and information they need to solve problems and make decisions.

Empowering mothers do the same thing. They know that the more they tell their kids what to do, the less their children learn to make good decisions and trust their instincts. Stella's children are grown now, but when they were young, she gave them challenging tasks to stretch their abilities and increase their self-confidence. She strove to step in with her two cents only when they needed it; otherwise, she backed off to allow them to figure things out on their own.

## Connect

Emotional connection is key to good leadership. Making strong connections demands the ability to regulate your emotions and empathize with others, and the emotional fortitude to know yourself and how your moods and actions affect others.

Lynn Bravewoman, a training specialist in a school district, is well liked by her coworkers and direct reports. As a union steward, even when she is seething with frustration, she monitors her behavior and stays calm, at least on the outside. In her union role, she needs to deal with highly emotional situations. She says that to do a good job requires that she listen well, gain rapport with others, establish trust, keep her own opinions and emotions in check, and exude self-confidence. It's no wonder she is next in line for union president.

Emotions can run high at Lynn's home as well. Her son, Sam, fourteen, says his mom takes the time to understand where he's coming from when he runs into a tough situation. Lynn stays close with Sam by using all the same skills she employs at work: listening, asking good questions, respecting points of view different from her own, and thinking before reacting. She has enough self-awareness to know when she is about to boil over, so she takes the time she needs before she says something she might later regret.

## Set an Example

The best leaders know that it's their behavior, not their words, that teaches the values they want to instill. Leaders see everyday situations as opportunities to demonstrate what they value.

Carol Evans, CEO of Working Mother Media, says she "walks the talk" when she encourages her employees to leave work at a reasonable hour so that they can spend time with their families, no matter how crazy things get at the office. At home, she established a "no work" zone, showing her kids how important it is to spend time together. The essential act of parenthood is to model behavior you want to see in your kids. If we want reliable kids, we need to act reliably. If we want respectful children, we must show respect. We teach our children through our acts, not our lectures.

◻ ◻ ◻

Any career woman has developed most of these skills at work. *Mom-in-Chief* will show you how to bring them home.

## HOW THIS BOOK WORKS

Each chapter in *Mom-in-Chief* presents workplace and family challenges that illustrate the connection between leadership at work and at home, and includes tools that help you apply leadership principles to your own challenges. The book takes you through seven essential strategies that address the gamut of leadership challenges; these strategies can work equally well in the business world and in family life:

Leadership Strategy 1: Setting Big-Picture Goals
Leadership Strategy 2: Discovering Your Leadership Style
Leadership Strategy 3: Managing Conflict
Leadership Strategy 4: Creating a Family Culture
Leadership Strategy 5: Leading Through Crisis
Leadership Strategy 6: Navigating the Growing Pains of Adolescence
Leadership Strategy 7: Balancing Priorities

Each of the five essential leadership skills are woven throughout each strategy and made practical and easy to apply to your unique situation with the help of assessment exercises and step-by-step action plans that help break through recurring conflicts, strengthen self-awareness, and keep your priorities straight.

Here are some common challenges:

> Should I make another dinner for my eight-year-old who rejected the pasta with the green stuff?
> Do I send my twenty-year-old son another hundred dollars after he lost the original hundred I sent him?
> How do I remain patient when I ask my five-year-old to get dressed for school for the fifth time?

These types of problems become more manageable once you understand how to clarify your desired outcomes and apply leadership skills to achieve goals.

Each chapter provides opportunities to reflect on your own situation and begin to take action. *Mom-in-Chief* will tackle such parenting issues as

- When to push kids and when to let them quit
- How to identify and break micromanaging habits
- How to navigate conflicts big and small
- When to "unprotect" children
- How to find the purpose behind the busy schedules

## WHO IS THIS BOOK FOR?

*Mom-in-Chief* is not about creating perfect little mini workplaces driven by hyperambitious parent-leaders. Nor is it about competing for the distinction of becoming the turbocharged family with high-performing children. Instead of exerting hypercontrol, assuming leadership means relaxing into an inner-directed, compassionate, noncompetitive mode. Leading a family doesn't mean churning out living masterpieces or indulging our children with the perfect everything. It means inspiring without pushing our own agenda, nurturing without being overly solicitous, challenging without aiming to win a best-of-show competition, expecting the best without ignoring the joyful ordinariness of childhood.

The good news is that moms demonstrate acts of leadership every day. We just need to remember to tap into our leader frame of mind instead of following the first impulse that our brain fires. We need to resist rescue missions and instead convey clear and firm expectations. We need strategies to maintain perspective when everything runs amok.

Although *Mom-in-Chief* focuses primarily on working mothers, I have interviewed many fathers, and I share stories from both men and women. I believe that the concepts in the book are useful to both moms and dads, as both play leadership roles in a child's life. That said, I felt drawn to the experience of motherhood and the unique challenges women face in terms of how we combine working and mothering in this culture.

Most parenting books focus on child development. *Mom-in-Chief* is about mom development. *Mom-in-Chief* addresses real quandaries, provides concrete strategies and meaningful assessment tools, and covers everything that smart, career-oriented women need to know in order to unleash their parenting potential and navigate challenges with skill and grace—without having to be a Supermom. *Mom-in-Chief* gives mothers the promotion they deserve. Finally!

# LEADERSHIP STRATEGY 1

# Setting Big-Picture Goals

> If we don't have the slightest clue about our hopes, dreams, and aspirations, then the chance that we'll take the lead is significantly less. In fact, we may not even see the opportunity that's right in front of us.
>
> —Jim Kouzes and Barry Posner, *The Leadership Challenge*

Kim G., a mother of two children and a customer service representative at Southwest Airlines (SWA), works for a company with a big-picture vision. SWA's guiding principle is that everyone in the company—from the president on down to the maintenance workers—pulls together to accomplish the airline's goal of great customer service.

As a supervisor, Kim tries to uphold the company's core value of respecting people and allowing employees to do what they need to do to get the job done. This isn't always easy when on some occasions her gut reaction is to reprimand her employees who make decisions that she herself wouldn't make, but she sticks to the company's big-picture vision.

Kim knows that only this atmosphere of collaboration and initiative can allow SWA employees to meet their core goals of affordability, customer service, and quick turnaround.

For instance, if a plane is late, everyone—the pilot and the ground crew—pitches in, bustling down the aisles and cleaning out the seat pockets. All employees, no matter what their job description or formal title, know that their first priority is to do whatever is necessary to get that plane turned around in fifteen minutes.

Kim only wished that things would run as smoothly at home. But with a husband who gets home late, and children who have busy elementary school schedules, the guiding principle in her household seemed to be chaos. She'd come home to find the kitchen piled with dishes, cat litter scattered on the floor, and four important things she had forgotten to do for the kids' school the next day. After maintaining her composure and equanimity all day at work, she'd find herself screaming at the kids—or at least the cat.

One evening, she arrived at home with only one hour until dinner guests were due to arrive. Everything seemed scattered and frazzled, and she was ready to suggest that they just go out to dinner or order in Chinese food. But instead she decided to try something she'd experienced that day at work, when the employees managed to turn around a late plane—with empty cups and newspapers strewn all over the seats—into an on-time departure just fifteen minutes later. She called her children into the kitchen and told them they were going to play an airplane game, where they had to get the house ready for the new passengers who were going to arrive in just half an hour. She told her daughter, Tricia, seven, that she could be captain. Todd, five, was the main flight attendant. They were going to do everything possible to pick up the mess and get the "plane" ready for company.

Instead of starting their usual whining when asked to do chores, the kids got into the airplane game immediately. Tricia put on a pilot's hat, and Todd spoke into his toy cell phone as if it were the plane's intercom. Soon they were scrambling around, picking up books and toys, and participating with enthusiasm— the same kind of cooperative spirit Kim usually only saw at work. By the time the guests arrived, the house was in order, the food was on the table, and everyone was cheerful.

Kim realized that what made her company work—sticking to its big-picture goals—could work at home too. She made time to sit down with her husband to talk about these goals, and they came up with their own big-picture parenting goal: to teach their children responsibility. Once they articulated this goal, they felt they could more easily set up a game plan for their household—allocating chores and sticking to them, having family meetings to recognize success, and refusing to do tasks the kids were perfectly capable of doing—that would make things run much more smoothly in the future and cultivate responsibility.

## SETTING CLEAR GOALS AT HOME

I begin most of my parenting seminars with a question: What are your primary goals or core values at home? Think big picture, beyond getting your kid to bathe every other day without screaming. Here are some typical responses:

"I want to raise a compassionate child."

"I want my child to be happy."

"I hope my kids find work that is meaningful and makes them happy."

"I want my partner and I to work together to raise our child in a loving and supportive environment."

"My biggest objective is for my children to think about the greater good and do their part to heal the world."

"I want my relationship to model what a relationship should be for a child as they grow up and have their own relationships."

"I want to give my children the room to discover who they truly are."

"I want to be free to discover who I truly am so I can provide the guidance, support, and modeling for my child to discover who he truly is."

Uplifting goals indeed! And that's just the point. Focusing on your big-picture goals elevates the daily grind into something more stimulating. Many moms in my seminars tell me they've never articulated these goals before. They can see, right away, the usefulness of defining their real objectives.

As one grantwriter put it, "I would never write a grant without a clearly articulated and compelling goal. It's funny that I worry about all sorts of relatively minor details at home, but I don't think about my overall goals."

Bingo. The challenge is to keep this mental picture in your mind as you drive the carpool, insist that the chores get done, and find yourself in the middle of a power struggle. When we don't set goals, we are susceptible to all sorts of enervating detours that take us away from where we want to go.

## REFOCUSING ON WHAT REALLY MATTERS

Workplaces across America are filled with cynical, burned-out people languishing in the meaninglessness of their workweek. The challenge for us all is to actively seek the meaning in our work, just as in other aspects of our lives. Helen, a customer service representative who answers the help line for a bank and won a customer service award, says she gets a lot of satisfaction from figuring out simple ways to explain complicated bank forms. The guy from AAA who fixed my flat tire says he gets a kick out of seeing the expressions of people stranded on the side of highways transform from anguished grimaces to smiles when he arrives. In contrast, the bad-tempered person who fixed my dead battery a couple of months later gave me every reason to believe he hated his job. Same job, different attitude. One saw his job in a broader context—that he's contributing to a person's safety and well-being—and the other saw his job as nothing more than a paycheck.

The reason goal setting is so important for business leaders and parents alike is that articulating a goal and committing to it focus our attention on the bigger meaning and inspire us not to lose our motivation over those niggling details.

## BIG-PICTURE DISCIPLINE

Kim at SWA was well aware that actions speak louder than a motto on an airplane napkin. The credibility of a vision or value statement is only as good as the actions that back them up, especially during difficult times. Let's look at how big-picture goals come to life (or don't) when your child misbehaves and your emotions cloud your vision.

### A Child's Revenge

Zachary, eleven, knew that his sister, Elissa, then nine, wanted a pony more than anything in the world. He nudged her awake at 7:30 in the morning, dragged her out of bed and down the stairs, and told her there was a big surprise for her in the backyard. Elissa believed that finally her dream had come true—a pony of her very own. But by the time she opened the sliding glass door leading to the backyard, Zach was laughing his head off. "Ha ha. April Fools!" Elissa, furious and devastated, ran back up into her bedroom and slammed the door.

When the tears stopped, she plotted her revenge. She knew what Zach liked more than anything: playing the piano. So that night she tiptoed into the bathroom, grabbed a jar, checked to see if the coast was clear, and sneaked into the living room to smear gobs of Vaseline over the keys of the grand piano. Once every last key was slimed, she returned the Vaseline to the bathroom and joined her parents in the kitchen, gleefully anticipating her brother's reaction when he went to play his adored piano.

So goes the story I heard my friend's daughter Elissa tell during her Bat Mitzvah. What hadn't occurred to Elissa in the heat of her vengeance was that she had ruined her family's prized grand piano. As she explained in her speech, the sweetness of revenge quickly soured when she saw the horror in her parents' eyes and realized the seriousness of her act.

I tell this story because there's no denying that Elissa misbehaved—big-time—and the situation would outrage any parent. Elissa felt vulnerable and ashamed. She knew her brother had triumphed with his pony shenanigans, and now he was, once again, the victor. Elissa's parents needed to discipline their daughter, but how?

The answer lies in focusing on the big picture. Great leaders and parents turn difficult situations into transforming teaching opportunities by keeping the ultimate goal in their mind's eye.

## Teachable Moments

Let's take a look at how Elissa's parents might respond. I'm sure you have comparable maddening stories and teachable moments in your life as a parent. How you respond to situations like these can accelerate your child's development . . . or simply invite a power struggle. It's just like when you're at the office and you hit a glitch. I've seen this pattern countless times: flailing businesses confront problems, turn them into crises, and then use the crisis as justification to abandon their long-range goals. They bounce from one strategy to another, people grow cynical, and each day feels like a slog. The best businesses, in contrast, run into just as many challenges, but instead of creating crises, they make it their job to understand what happened, learn all they can, and commit to different actions that will help them get to the same end goal.

## Ineffective Responses

Strong leadership is hard to pull off when your best employee fails to deliver. How about when you're furious about your child's misbehavior? Let's look at a few possible responses:

1. "You ruined the piano! What in the world were you thinking?! How could you be so irresponsible and thoughtless?"

2. "You're grounded. Go to your room and think about what you did and how you're going to pay to get our piano repaired."

3. "Elissa, you must have been very angry at your brother. Do you want to talk about it?"

When we think about our own angry, knee-jerk reactions, the first two responses are understandable. In the long run, however, all three of these responses obstruct your higher purpose: to raise a respectful child who checks her impulses and is sensitive to the consequences of her actions. And here's another big-picture goal to keep in mind during any difficult interaction with your child: to maintain a supportive, loving connection.

### Labeling

The first response—labeling—sets up a dangerous outcome because it imposes a fixed view of Elissa as irresponsible and thoughtless, undermining her motivation to improve. Elissa is apt to think, *If I'm seen as irresponsible, then there's nothing I can do to change your view of me (and worse, my view of myself)*. According to this mindset, she might as well smear the rest of the furniture in the house. Too often, we act as though our children's misbehavior indicates an unchangeable character flaw. If her parents had reacted this way, Elissa would be well on her way to considering herself irresponsible, insensitive, and overly emotional.

One of the worst aspect of labels is that they are self-fulfilling and therefore inhibit improvement. I see this phenomenon in the workplace all the time: the boss, disappointed in some aspect of the employee's behavior, labels him a weak performer. Having set this low expectation, the boss then views the employee with a lack of trust and with little confidence in the employee's abilities. The employee grows apathetic, throwing up his hands and saying, "Nothing I do will change her view of me, so why try?"

We can get locked in to the same self-reinforcing cycle with our children. Obviously when we're furious because our child ruined a prized possession, only a robot-mom can react calmly, but it's important to learn how to express your authentic feelings while not letting your anger humiliate or degrade your child. You can say, for example, "I am so furious and upset about this," without adding the blame and labeling—"What in the world were you thinking?! What an awful, irresponsible girl you are." Adding to Elissa's self-criticism would only rob her of exactly what she needed to learn from this experience—that she could remedy the situation and still be seen as a good person worthy of her family's love. The trick is to convey the message that Elissa is a good, responsible girl who made a bad choice.

### Immediate Punishment

The second reaction, immediate punishment, denies Elissa the opportunity to come up with her own consequences—and remedies. Grounding her right away and telling her to pay for the piano give her no chance to make amends, because the remedy (paying for repairs) was not her idea. Clearly, a consequence is appropriate, but imposing it this way allows Elissa no chance to earn back her self-respect or the respect of her parents. What's more, this tactic will likely perpetuate her feeling of being wronged. A much better approach, especially for an older child, is to include her in establishing a consequence. Adults and children alike are more likely to buy into a solution if they participate in creating it.

### Inauthentic Talk

The third reaction—"Let's talk"—makes sense on the surface but lacks an authentic edge. There is a time for listening and talking, but the first order of business is to convey a strong message that this act is outside the zone of acceptable behavior. Your true feelings, whether sadness or anger, send your child a clear and ultimately helpful message that when she acts in certain ways, her behavior elicits a strong and human reaction. Too many parents bend over backwards to protect their children from anything unpleasant, abdicating their leadership. Barbara Waterman, Ph.D., a child psychologist, sees many parents who are reluctant to critique their child's behavior in a strong, steady way. When parents neglect opportunities to correct misbehavior, they miss opportunities to teach empathy and morality.

"To instill morality, you need to instill a positive form of guilt, which is very different from shaming them for their misbehavior," says Dr. Waterman. "Guilt can be good. When kids do wrong, they feel guilt, triggered by thoughts of their parent's disapproval, and that guilt allows them to self-correct their behavior."

I tell bosses all the time that creating some discomfort prompts behavior change. Too many times, I see managers who sugarcoat feedback or shy away from giving hard-hitting feedback, wanting to be popular. They only foster mediocrity. The same thing can happen at home.

### The Big-Picture Response

What Elissa's parents, Michelle and Lorne, did was express how upset they were, making it clear they disapproved. They could see from Elissa's face how ashamed she was. They acknowledged their authentic reaction—disappointment—but resisted the urge to go a step further and humiliate or criticize her.

Later, when everyone's emotions settled down, they had a long talk with Elissa about being more aware of how her actions affect others. They also talked about Elissa's chronic frustration with her brother and made clear to Zach that his teasing had to stop. They listened and validated Elissa's hurt feelings that compelled her to get even. Michelle and Lorne discussed with Elissa other ways she could have expressed her anger more appropriately.

"I was so grateful my parents didn't take their anger out on me. They knew it wasn't my intention to ruin the piano," says Elissa.

If you discipline with respect, your child will respond by trying to win your approval. If you try to correct misbehavior through humiliation, your child is more likely to retaliate. Good leaders cultivate mutual trust.

At her Bat Mitzvah, Elissa spoke about how her big mistake gave her an occasion to learn the limits of revenge and how reacting in the heat of the moment led her to do something that she later regretted. She realized how terrible it feels to disappoint people you love. Her parents could have come down on her hard, with punishments and harsh judgments. Although that approach would have been understandable (and admittedly, I've criticized my kids for far more minor infractions), Elissa's parents saw that the situation presented a defining leadership moment, which they used to full advantage. It wasn't that they didn't seethe with frustration over the experience, but Michelle and Lorne had the wherewithal to give Elissa room to reflect, take responsibility for her actions, learn that her choices have consequences, and grow.

## PROMOTING GROWTH

Transformational leadership is fueled by a deep belief that children and adults are works in progress, and will, if given guidance and trust, learn from their mistakes, change, and grow. Great leaders both at work and at home act with a mindset that says, "You are a person capable of growth, and my job is to figure out creative ways to nurture your development. I will help you learn from your mistakes and give you the unconditional acceptance to recover from failures and get back on track." With this mindset, you're constantly on the lookout for opportunities to promote growth.

### Failure as Opportunity

The most effective leaders know that the biggest growth opportunities come at times of failure. Sadly, most people become *bosses*, not *leaders*, wielding power when things go badly. Failure brings the perfect lessons for positive development *if* you reject the belief that failure indicates some innate character trait and *if* you view failure as a path to mastery.

For great leaders, mistakes are inspiring because they motivate people to take a look in the mirror and think about how they can improve and hit their mark the next time. These leaders see it as their job to help people dispel the notion that failure means that there is something innately inferior in them. Failure becomes a stepping-stone to success.

I worked with an executive, Harriet, who was embroiled in a power struggle with her budget manager, Randy. All had been fine between them until Randy made a budgeting error that threw the company into a deficit. From that point on, Harriet collected ammunition to justify her view of Randy—that he was careless and lacked the detail orientation and analytical skills required for the job. The bottom line: she was determined to fire Randy.

Randy launched a job search and, after five months, landed a job in a Fortune 500 company three times the size of his former company. One year later, he rose to the position of chief financial officer, managing a multimillion-dollar budget.

Randy looks back on his former boss with disdain but also amazement.

"I can see now in retrospect the power her view of me had on my performance. I really thought I was not cut out for this type of work. I believed I lacked some inborn quality that other successful finance people possessed."

## The Growth Mindset

Randy's reaction wouldn't surprise Stanford's Carol Dweck, author of *Mindset: The New Psychology of Success*. In her research, she showed that people succeed or fail based on whether they have a fixed or growth mindset. With a fixed mindset, you believe that success is due to inborn abilities. If you hold a growth mindset, you believe that success comes from practice, hard work, and a readiness to persevere after failure. Harriet labeled Randy as inadequate and irredeemable and that led to his fixed view of himself. The good news is that the fixed view can be reversed under the right conditions.

The dangers of a fixed mindset are significant for parents. You inadvertently embrace the fixed mindset when you praise your child's intelligence, athleticism, or artistry. I fall into this myself: when Leah won a poetry contest, I said, "You're such a good poet!" or after Anna's karaoke rendition of "Bohemian Rhapsody," I said, "You are a great singer." Kids get the message that being smart or talented at something is simply inbred, not the result of effort. The consequence: kids avoid taking risks for fear that if they fail, they'll lose their coveted label. And why try hard? Being smart, athletic, or artistic shouldn't require hard work if it's innate.

A growth mindset, in contrast, brings huge benefits. If you hold a growth mindset, you convey messages that success takes practice and that setbacks are part of the journey to achievement, not proof of inherent flaws. In one of Carol's experiments with junior high schoolers, her research team told half the students that their brains are like muscles that can be developed with exercise and that the math would be hard initially but then, with practice, would get easier. Sure enough, the kids who were given growth mindset messages significantly outperformed their peers.

When your kids say, "Keegan's a good artist" or "I'm bad at math," they are holding a fixed mindset about themselves and others. This view comes naturally to them (and us), so it's our job as parents to combat such thinking with messages like, "Keegan's mom tells me that Keegan practices sketching for hours after school each day" or "Math doesn't come easily for anyone. It takes a lot of hard work and practice."

Another way to conquer a fixed mindset is to foster a healthy respect for mistakes. I like to tell my kids what I call failure success stories to help them see that even their heroes encountered failure first. My daughter Anna's favorite story: the Beatles were turned down by a recording company because the executive didn't like their sound and said that their type of music was on its way out. Charles Shultz, the creator of the *Peanuts* comic strip, was turned down by his high school yearbook. Albert Einstein failed his first college entrance exam, and Dr. Seuss's books were rejected by publisher after publisher. Failure success stories teach children a powerful lesson: success comes only after lots and lots of effort and perseverance.

I advise work teams to make a habit of sharing their mistakes and discussing what they learned as a result. You can do the same at home. In her role as executive director of UC Berkeley's Greater Good Science Center, Christine Carter, Ph.D., studies what makes children happy. At the dinner table at home, she regularly asks her two daughters, ages five and seven, to share what mistakes they made and, if they can, to talk about something they learned from them. This, she says, is a great way to promote the growth mindset.

## STICKING WITH YOUR GOALS

The best business leaders have clearly defined the results they want to achieve. They set goals and ask themselves, What must I do each day to support my goals and lead to my desired outcomes? Goals drive success, but we all know people who constantly articulate goals but don't stick to them. There are several essential things to keep in mind to make sure that your goals turn into actions that in turn lead to desired results.

### Making Your Goals Vivid

The clearer your mental picture of your desired outcomes, the more likely you are to behave in a way that supports your goals. For example, if on New Year's Eve I announce my resolution—to become more physically fit—I know the likely outcome.

I'll exercise like crazy for a few weeks and then go back to my old ways. If I really want to sustain positive change, there are three secrets I need to follow:

1. **Keep a vivid picture in mind.** The image of hiking in the mountains with my kids into my old age keeps me on my exercise routine. Sometimes it's a picture of my maternal grandmother hunched over with osteoporosis that gets me out of bed and on the hiking trail. It's best if your picture includes the benefit of achieving your goal as well as the costs of not reaching it.

2. **Chart out the specifics.** I'm going to hike on Monday, Wednesday, and Friday mornings on the trails a mile from my house. Announcing to your coworkers that you're going to join a gym won't cut it.

3. **Enlist support.** I'll invite my friend Diane to join me; she'll motivate me and keep me, literally and figuratively, on my path. The more friends you enlist—the more people with whom you share your goal—the deeper your accountability and the greater your chance of following through.

Once you establish a crystal-clear intention, you have set up a clear accountability for yourself with a goal that is easy to track and measure. If I have defined "physically fit" as hiking three times each week, I can't get away with saying, Hey, look at me, I'm more fit now—I get up to change the TV channel instead of using a remote. This approach works the same way on the job. If you have clear, measurable goals, you're far more likely to get where you're aiming to go than if you say something vague like, "We are going to provide better customer service this year."

For example, I worked with an organization that was losing customers like crazy. In a poll, customers said they didn't like the surly service at the retail outlets. Profits were at an all-time low. The fear of bankruptcy had everyone on edge. The company needed a specific strategy for change, achieved through concrete goals. Management began by asking simple but essential questions: What does better customer service look like? How will you know you're providing better service (in other words, How will you measure progress?)? Be more courteous? Great, but one person's courteous is different from another's. What does courteous *look* like and *sound* like? We smile, make eye contact with customers, help people find what they're looking for by walking them to the merchandise, return phone calls and e-mails within three hours . . . Now you have something concrete to measure, and you're on your way to real improvement.

Likewise, with parenting, it helps to define, specifically, what you *do* when you are a big-picture parent. What do you do to motivate, empower, set an example, connect, and focus on the big picture? Try committing to just one or two specific actions to support your big-picture goals and develop as a leader at home and at work.

Big-picture parenting requires articulating your higher purpose and acting in alignment with your highest priorities. But it all starts with a big-picture *mindset.* I want to share with you a parable that powerfully brings home the importance of creating a clear mental picture of your higher purpose:

> One day I came across three bricklayers. I asked the first bricklayer what he was doing.
>
> "Laying bricks," he told me.
>
> I asked the second what he was doing.
>
> "Making a brick wall," he told me.
>
> I asked the third what he was doing.
>
> "Building a cathedral," he explained with a smile.

It is more the rule than the exception that the leaders I meet at home and at work are unclear about why they are doing what they're doing each day. Their sights are restricted to merely doing tasks (laying bricks); they don't see how the bricks fit into the big picture. Similarly, if we as parents don't stop to reflect on the big picture, we are simply getting through each day with no sense of progress toward a larger goal.

## DEFINING CONCRETE GOALS

Take a few moments to write your thoughts about the following questions. Think of two or three specific actions you want to commit to in order to support each of your three goals. Ideally, these actions represent something you want to do differently from what you're doing now. For example, if your primary parenting goal is to raise happy children, you might want to commit to actions that will enhance your own happiness and help you become a living example of your goal.

1. What is your primary parenting goal?
2. What is your primary career goal?
3. What is your primary relationship goal?

Once your articulate your goals and several actions to support them, go through the following checklist:

☐　Does each goal give you a clear mental picture of what success will look like?

☐　Do the actions move you toward your mental picture of success?

☐　Have you enlisted people who will help keep you on track? Have you shared your goals with these people and specified what you need from them to support your goals?

## Keeping Focused on Your Goals

It's hard to pack a healthy lunch for your kids, get to work each day, conduct coherent discussions with colleagues, come home and keep your cool when your children are tired and cranky—when you're tired and cranky yourself—and still stay focused on your long-term goals. This is the challenge of leadership at home and at work. There are three strategies that help keep you focused on your big picture:

1. Stay self-aware and accountable.
2. Pursue *your* dreams.
3. Keep your priorities straight.

### Stay Self-Aware and Accountable

Every parent I've ever talked to has experienced moments when they stop in their tracks and say, "I can't believe I said—thought, did—that."

Last month, I had an eye-opening lesson with a violin. Anna, my now thirteen-year-old, forgot her instrument on the city bus. When she got home from school, the phone rang. It was her friend Julian. He had noticed that she had left her violin behind and took it home. I thanked Julian profusely and hung up the phone.

The forgotten violin came after a long string of lost jackets, watches, and bus passes. I was at the end of my rope. Instead of saying something like, "Don't feel bad—Yo Yo Ma forgot his $2.5 million cello in the trunk of a New York City taxicab once," I said in my Wicked Witch of the West voice, "I hope you take this as a lesson and never forget your violin again." I went on, reminding her how expensive replacing the violin would have been and what if Julian hadn't saved the day, and she needed to stop being so scatterbrained, etc., etc., etc.

Maya Angelou said, "You can tell a lot about a person by how they deal with lost luggage." Moms deal with the equivalent of lost luggage every day. What if I responded to life's nuisances with a sense of calm? What if "goddammit" hadn't leapt from my lips when Anna left her violin on the bus? Keeping perspective is a pretty tall order, especially when I'm having one of my short-on-patience days.

When Anna left her violin on the bus, could I lighten up because, as leadership consultant Tom Peters says, excellent failures bring excellent learning? What would happen if I responded without judgment, if finger wagging transformed, somehow—breathe-breathe—into a hug? Could Anna learn to treat her own mistakes with compassion?

During Anna's confession, her tears and quivering bottom lip told the whole story. If I continued with my heavy-handed approach every time she made a mistake, I might drive Anna to hide her mistakes from me. What am I teaching her when I'm critical—to be self-critical, guilty, impatient with herself and others? My big-picture goals were just the opposite. I wanted Anna to be self-respecting, forgiving, and compassionate. Anna was fully equipped to learn her own lesson. All I needed was to firmly but calmly (no spewing, no humiliation) share my feelings and then get out of the way and give her the space and support to learn and grow. I could have said something like, "It makes me nervous that you left your violin. I can see you feel awful about it, but I do need your commitment that you'll be more careful with it."

Many workplaces, especially the successful ones, conduct some form of failure analysis to build self-awareness and accountability. Hospitals routinely use morbidity and mortality conferences to analyze, understand, and learn from mistakes. The U.S. Army is known for conducting after-action reviews to analyze and learn from their successes and failures. Barclays Global Investors calls mistakes process improvement opportunities. Are you prepared to conduct a failure analysis on yourself when you mess up?

Promoting personal accountability means asking your-self how you contributed to the setback or mistake (or, in my case, made a mistake worse by failing to seize an opportunity to promote growth). This crucial question gets to the heart of accountability—honest and deep reflection. Even if you're only 5 percent responsible compared to your coworker's, spouse's, or child's 95 percent, you have far more capability to change your own behavior than someone else's. It's not about condemn-ing yourself each time your temper flares when you're trying to get your kids out the door to school. Staying self-aware and accountable is about making a habit of listening to yourself and watching your behavior and its impact on others so that you build your leadership muscles every day.

It's hard to shift from finding handy excuses to looking inward. Easier to say, "You made me so angry" or "It's your fault I lost my cool" than to take a more accountable position: "What triggered my anger, and how can I better regulate my anger next time?" or "What part of this problem can I take responsibility for and learn from, so that I can change my behavior the next time?" (You'll learn more about how to foster accountability in yourself and your children in Leadership Strategy 4.)

Staying self-aware and accountable takes practice. You can say, "I'm a hothead. It's just the way I am"—good fixed mind-set thinking—or you can commit to practicing self-awareness, responding to difficult situations in ways that get you closer to your big-picture goals.

### Pursue Your Dreams

The most enjoyable and powerful way to live with your big picture in mind and take your parenting, job performance, marital satis-faction, and personal fulfillment up a notch is to pursue your *non-mom* goals. This may seem counterintuitive, so let me explain.

When Anna was barely four and Leah was born, I was all mom, through and through. But after the excuse of sheer exhaustion of a newborn wore off, there were several more years when I aban-doned hiking, reading, bicycling, writing, seeing movies, and more than a few friends. A new friend I met at a work conference, Erica, a single mom, manager of a medical department in a university, and opera singer on the side, asked me what my passion was as a non-mom.

I drew a blank. I made something up from my past.

"Writing," I said unconvincingly.

"What do you write?" she asked.

"I'm on hiatus," I said. But I couldn't leave that feeling that I had lost part of myself. A mom of a friend of Anna's had said to me once that her life was on hold until her kids were grown. Was I doing the same thing?

I met Clara Alvarez, twenty-seven, a welfare recipient and mother of two toddlers, while coaching the leadership team at the Merced County Human Services Agency. Clara told me that she felt shame collecting welfare. She went to school at night, held down three jobs, slept five hours each night, and still barely managed to pay her bills. I asked her what kept her going each day. She said that she got her strength from realizing that her children wouldn't fulfill their dreams if she didn't pursue hers.

"I lie in bed every night and decide that the next day will be one step closer to getting out of this mess and living a life I know I and my kids are worthy of living," said Clara. She was able to look forward to a time when all the hard work would be worth it.

In coaching leaders, one of the first lessons I teach is this: to perform your best and inspire the best in others, you need to step back from the pressure and nurture yourself. Whether we are running a company or a carpool, when we don't take a breather and focus on our non-mom selves, our joy is too often displaced by feelings of resentment and pointless drudgery. How can we expect our children to pursue their dreams when we defer our own? If you're like most parents, you want to raise a happy, self-respecting child who pursues her passions. One of the most powerful ways you can do that is to be a living example of a person who finds happiness in pursuing her own dreams.

### Keep Your Priorities Straight

My mom, a single mother and schoolteacher, had a picture on the refrigerator of a woman on a chair, recoiling from a vacuum cleaner below. The caption said, "Inordinate fear of housework."

We had a saying in our house—"Soak your way to freedom"—which justified the piles of dirty dishes. I know this view of housework was unconventional, but it taught me an important lesson. The untouched dirty dishes meant, for a working mom like mine, that we could enjoy a Scrabble game or cuddle up on the couch watching *Rhoda*.

I try to remember my "soak your way to freedom" lesson: the dishes can wait. The e-mail can wait. When I'm tired, when I'm frustrated, when I reach a wall, I need to take a breath, drop the compulsion to clean, to cook, and, the hardest one for me, to check e-mail.

Barbara Leslie, a lobbyist who works long hours, let go of home improvements so that she could focus on priorities more important to her and her family. She loves her job and enjoys family time, but the thought of remodeling put her and her husband over the edge.

"We've had paint swatches on our bedroom walls for over four years, broken light fixtures for five years, holes in the walls, and no door knobs. Our bedsheets are so threadbare that my husband's feet ripped right through them the other night. It's bad. But we take great family vacations and eat dinners together. It's all about setting clear priorities," says Barbara.

It's standard operating procedure for working moms to live out of alignment with their priorities. We're just too busy, too tired, and too overwhelmed. Here are some examples of out-of-sync parenting. Any sound familiar?

"I wanted to go on a family camping trip, but had to cancel because of my relentless workload."

"I know family dinners are important, but rounding up my four kids is like herding kittens. I can't manage to get everyone at home and fed at the same time."

"I scream at my kids on a daily basis. I don't mean to, but when they don't listen to me, I finally just lose my head."

## OBSTACLES TO BIG-PICTURE PLANNING

There are myriad seductive detours that steer working mothers away from the ultimately more rewarding big picture. Let's explore the top two detours: self-sacrifice and micromanaging.

### Self-Sacrifice

It takes courage and discipline to check your impulses and rearrange your calendar. The first thing you can do to clear the path to your big-picture goals is to find ways to rejuvenate. The path of least resistance for many working mothers I talk to is to bend to the boss's pressure and work through the weekend. Are you one of these moms? On the edge of collapse, you still shuttle the kids to and from soccer; schedule the orthodontist, dentist, and doctor's appointments; and plan birthday parties. Your husband becomes a source of resentment—can't he take some of this on? You don't dare ask, because he can't do it properly (you remember the time he delivered the kids to school without brushing their hair or their teeth), and besides, he works night and day also. This becomes your normal way of being—pulling the double shift, snapping at your husband and your kids, abandoning the hobbies you used to enjoy—but it's not healthy or sustainable. Your Good Mom expectations grab you by the heart and pull you into a myopic whirlwind of activity.

Here's the paradox: we avoid pursuing our more ambitious big-picture goals to make life "easier" today. It's easier to do the chores yourself than negotiate a shared load with your partner or engage in a battle with your four-year-old. It's simpler to make a second dinner when your toddler pushes away the green pesto. And another paradox: we deny ourselves nurturing pleasures that we enjoyed in our pre-mom days—the romantic date, the shopping spree, the walk around the lake—only to realize that we're miserable. It's so simple, it's a cliché: when Mom's not happy, no one's happy. You set the tone. You are the role model. You are the leader. If you feel like the resident butler, let it be a clue to you that you're not doing anyone a favor—not you, not your partner, and not your kids. When you're forward-looking, you recognize that how you live your life will influence how your kids live their lives.

### Micromanaging

Closely related to self-sacrifice is micromanaging. Great leaders step back and let their followers assume responsibility. They delegate. They set an example. They motivate. They empower.

---

### EIGHT REASONS WHY YOU DON'T DELEGATE

1. It takes too much time to explain the task; it's easier and faster to do it yourself.
2. Only you can do the task properly.
3. You enjoy being in control.
4. You enjoy feeling needed and important.
5. You worry that your children are too busy.
6. You want to be nice and shoulder the burdens yourself.
7. You enjoy your martyrdom.
8. You are unwilling to let others make mistakes.

As a manager, I delegated like crazy. Why do it myself when someone else could gain valuable experience from doing it? But at home, it's a different story. Why? Through some potent mixture of guilt, worry, self-importance, and need for control, I feel compelled to do it all. I brushed my daughter Anna's hair until she was twelve because I could do it better and she needed me. I bus the table when Leah whines that she has to get to her homework. I suggest 101 things my kids can do when they're bored before I catch myself and say, wait, you need to figure out how to amuse yourselves without my help. I fix snacks, pack lunches, search out lost library books. I am Supermom. I am Superwife while my husband lounges in front of the TV watching soccer matches. OK—he actually does a lot, especially when I back off—but micromanaging brings on a bitter martyr complex that distorts my view of my husband in unflattering ways. Intellectually I know that the more I do things for Anna and Leah that they can do for themselves, the more dependent they become and the more they feel *entitled* to a mom who runs around serving them. When I take it all on myself, when I insist that I need to take the kids clothes shopping, for example, and that my husband couldn't possibly navigate the preteen clothes department, I'm leaving Burke in the dark about Leah's taste for stretchy waistlines and Anna's desire for well-fitting jeans. All it takes is one shopping trip, and he's up to speed. So why don't I relinquish that chore? My actions are in direct conflict with my long-term parenting goal to raise responsible, self-reliant children and to model collaboration—look kids: mommies and daddies share the domestic load.

Resisting the temptations of micromanagement yields amazing results: employees and children who feel respected, assume responsibility, and take initiative; who demonstrate willingness to engage in trial-and-error learning; and who experience the self-confidence to think independently. When you've hit a wall of exhaustion and you decide that delegation

## DELEGATION QUIZ

Take the following quiz to determine how well you delegate at home and at work. Circle yes or no.

1. Do you take back the task you've delegated at the first sign of mistakes?　　Yes　　No

2. Do you find yourself working in your office long after others have gone home?　　Yes　　No

3. Do you think things will fall apart when you're not there?　　Yes　　No

4. Do you do tasks others are perfectly capable of doing?　　Yes　　No

5. Do people do the tasks you've assigned only after you've nagged them?　　Yes　　No

If you circled yes for two or more questions, it's time to take a hard look at improving your delegation skills. Look at delegation as an opportunity to build trust, gain time, and foster responsibility.

is your way to liberation and a happier family life, here are the steps you can take:

**Decide to whom you will delegate.** Balance the level of challenge and the types of tasks with the person's interests and skills. The best leaders focus not just on getting the job done but also on how to create motivating conditions; this means finding the right level of challenge, providing needed training, and giving recognition so that people feel appreciated.

**Decide what to delay.** Learn to let go, say no, and do it only
when it's a "must-do" and aligned with your big-picture
goals.

**Assign the task.** Specify what is involved, when the task needs to
be done, and what challenges the person might encounter. Put
the task in context—how will the task contribute to the household or organization? Who will be helped when the task is done
(or hurt if the task isn't completed)?

**Follow up.** Ask for progress reports, check in to see how it's
going, offer support, allow for setbacks, say thank you, and
recognize success.

## DEVELOPING FAMILY CORE VALUES

In every healthy workplace I've ever worked, employees know
what the core values are—customer service, quality, innovation,
cost-effectiveness, and so on. These core values are important
because they guide behavior—they help people make choices
about how to spend their time and money, and clarify what
behavior gets praised, condoned, or penalized. Why not achieve
clarity and buy-in on the core values of your family?

Here are some interactive steps you can take to establish
your family's core values. Your family may resist at first, but soon
will find this to be a fun, powerful tool to help create the family
you want.

1. Get a big sheet of paper, ideally the size of a flipchart. Tape
   it on the wall. Draw a big circle on the paper.

2. Decide who will be the scribe. Then get kids, spouse, and
   other family members engaged right off the bat by asking
   everyone to call out what they know about Disneyland,
   a culture and organization that nearly everyone admires
   and enjoys. Give some examples to start them off: fun
   rides, crowded, clean, friendly customer service. Once you

have all filled the page with ideas, share the four official core Disneyland values: (1) courtesy, (2) safety, (3) show (characters, rides, building, all the things that contribute to the Disney "magic"), and (4) efficiency.

3. Next, draw a circle on a fresh sheet of paper. Now it's time to describe your family as you really see it. Again provide a few examples: we eat dinner together, do lots of chores, volunteer on clean-up days at the local creek. Then ask everyone to share his or her thoughts.

4. Ask for ideas that may not describe your family now, but that you'd like to see in the future, such as travel to foreign countries or lots of time playing games.

5. Keep in mind that every idea is valid. Don't evaluate, even if your child says, "Watch TV all day." Remember, this is a fun activity.

6. Ask everyone to look over the list and come up with your three or four core family values—for example, fun, outdoorsy, hard working.

7. Now talk about how you could make your core values come alive; for example, how do you treat each other, and how do you spend your time?

Post the sheet on a wall so that you can go back to it, talk about it, and modify it as the mood hits. Carve out time during dinner to come up with ideas to make each core value come to life.

## CREATING A PARENTING MISSION STATEMENT

A powerful tool to promote your commitment to big-picture parenting is to craft a parenting mission statement. If you co-parent, talk together about what kinds of qualities you want your children to have when they're grown.

When my husband and I began to talk about our parenting principles, we started with three big-picture goals: to instill joy in learning, to build a strong family connection, and to promote a focus on the greater good. Little by little, we came up with ideas to fulfill these goals. For example:

- We chose books to read together and made the effort to get to bed earlier to make plenty of time for reading.
- I started a mother-daughter book group with some friends.
- When we went on trips, we read books about our destinations.
- We talked about the current community, national, and world events at the dinner table.
- We decided on community service activities we could do as a family—for example, cleaning up local creeks and participating in walkathons to raise money for causes we care about.

To create a parenting mission statement, begin by imagining that your children are grown. Reflect on the following questions in terms of your *ideal* vision:

1. What do your children say about their relationship with you?
2. What do they most admire about you? What parental and nonparental accomplishments or qualities do they admire in you?
3. What do they say about their family's strongest values?
4. What do your children value most?
5. What memorable family experiences do they recount?

Now ask yourself, What do we need to *do* to make our ideal vision a reality?

Another helpful exercise in crafting a parenting mission statement is to consider the qualities you hope your children will demonstrate throughout their lives. As you gaze ahead into the future ten to twenty years, what are your hopes for your children? What do you admire most about them? Decide which five qualities you think would be the most important. For example: Our children are

- Successful, yet considerate of others
- Passionate about their dreams, yet not self-absorbed
- Connected to family, yet they contribute to the greater good
- Always ready to stand up for what's right, yet respect differences
- Able to take risks, yet do not feel defeated by failures

Talk with family members about creative ways to make your mission statement come alive instead of having it end up just sitting on the bedside table underneath your pile of books. Some parents post mission statements on the kitchen wall and use them as springboards for family discussions. One parent couple reviews their mission statement the first Sunday of each month and assesses whether their actions and the way they spend their time reinforce or undermine their mission statement. The process of developing a mission statement is beneficial in and of itself, but can be even more transforming if you regularly monitor and discuss the mission.

☐☐☐

Being a mother brings endless chores and head-spinning logistics. When we are deluged with countless menial tasks, whiny requests, and several daily servings of frustration, it's easy to lose sight of the bigger picture. Let's face reality: someone has to do the laundry. Revisiting your goals can ease the daily frustrations. Write down your goals and keep them on your bedside table or in your wallet. Glance at them from time to time and let them guide your actions. When you've aligned your core values with your daily choices and actions, life at home, for both you and your family, will improve drastically. What you *do*—how you promote a growth mindset, stay self-aware and accountable, pursue your dreams, and keep your priorities straight—keeps you on the big-picture parenting path.

In the next chapter, you'll learn how you express your big-picture goals through your personal leadership style. You'll take a self-assessment to gain insight about your "Mom Mode." When you play to your strengths and values, you get better results and feel more satisfied as a parent. Understanding your Mom Mode will also shed light on why you and your partner sometimes can't see eye to eye.

# Discovering Your Leadership Style

Sometimes when I watch my friend Susan, whose kids are all super-stars, I wonder if I'm parenting the right way.

One of Susan's kids is traveling to Kyrgyzstan—or was is Kazakhstan?—to sing in her choir. Another of her kids is criss-crossing all over California, winning enough trophies and ribbons to reach clear across Kyrgyzstan, and the youngest, age nine, has already danced in four *Nutcrackers*.

I think to myself, why couldn't I be that kind of mother? How does Susan do it? All that pressure and driving and success, so early. My brain wanders over to a vision of my kids lying zombie-like on the couch, watching their umpteenth episode of *Sabrina the Teenage Witch*, and my stomach clenches. I blew it, I think. I've messed up their chances for a more promising future. I've malnourished their burgeoning talent. Of course, the reality is that my kids don't actu-ally watch *Sabrina* all day. In fact, they have plenty of interests and talents, but parental insecurity does a number on logic, and voilá, before I know it, I've concluded that I Am a Bad Mom.

## BEING THE MOM YOU ARE

It's taken me some time to get over this kind of thinking, but I've realized that I'm really not such a Bad Mom at all, nor will I ever be a mother like my friend Susan.

Every mom, like every business leader, has her own personal style that showcases her strengths and inspires those around her. I call these styles Mom Modes, the skills and strategies that build relationships, encourage individuality, and promote success. The three basic modes are

- Achiever
- Connector
- Liberator

If you recognize and respect your own Mom Mode—and don't compare yourself to others—you'll be more effective and satisfied as a parent. One is not better than another as long as you stay true to yourself and your mode. There's lots of room for your own distinct style within each mode, but you can use the Mom Modes as shorthand to better understand your attitudes and behaviors as well as those of your co-parent and the other parents in your child's life. In this chapter, I'll show you how to discover your Mom Mode.

When you are yourself, authentically you, you can drop the self-judgment and the second-guessing. When you operate from your Mom Mode, making the right choices that match your parenting values and not someone else's, you've won any competition, hands down.

You can develop your transformational leadership skills by first becoming aware of what your preferred style of leadership is, enabling you to leverage your natural strengths and feel more joy and success in what you do. Your Mom Mode translates into your behaviors every day—how you talk to your child, how you foster or suppress initiative, and how you promote independent thinking and inspire success. Knowing your Mom Mode helps you amplify your unique strengths and passions, and discard behaviors that stunt the transformational process. With a deeper wisdom about your personal leadership style, you will be better equipped to bring out the best in yourself so that you and your kids can thrive.

## DISCOVERING YOUR MOM MODE

Before I describe in more detail the three Mom Modes, let's determine yours. When you take the Mom Mode assessment, think about who you *truly* are, not who you think you should be. You are likely to feel that all three choices characterize you, but try to rank them according to which choice *best* describes you now. Even though we operate from each of the modes, there is typically one that is dominant. Go with your first instinct as you answer the questions. Resist the temptation to over think your response. You may shake your head saying, "I can't rank one of these answers over another." Try. There are no wrong answers. Now take a moment to complete the assessment (p. 50).

## MOM MODE ASSESSEMENT

**Instructions:**

Rank the words in each row (left to right, **not vertically**). Place a **3** in the box that **best characterizes** you in your parenting role, a 2 in the box that somewhat characterizes you, and a 1 in the box that least characterizes you. **Each box will have one number, a 1, 2, *or* 3 (no ties!).** Don't overthink your responses. Be honest. Don't respond in the way that you feel is socially desirable. There are no good or bad responses. **Remember: 3 BEST characterizes you, and 1 LEAST characterizes you.** Respond in the context of your parenting role.

|   |   | **A** | **B** | **C** |
|---|---|---|---|---|
| 1 | I most value for my child . . . | Achievement | Emotional connection | Individuality |
| 2 | My most important role as a parent is to . . . | Foster individuality | Build close connection | Unleash potential |
| 3 | I'm most likely to say . . . | Strive for success | Be yourself | Build healthy relationships |
| 4 | My top priority as a parent is to . . . | Encourage intimacy | Foster independent thinking | Encourage growth |
| 5 | I most want my child to . . . | Be emotionally aware | Be true to self | Seek challenge |
| 6 | Potential parental challenge for me: | Overreacting | Pushing too hard | Providing emotional support |
| 7 | As a parent, I tend to be impatient with . . . | Conformity | Apathy | Insensitivity |
| 8 | As a parent, I can be . . . | Competitive | Overinvolved | Remote |

## Scoring:

Transfer the numbers (3, 2, 1) that you wrote in each square. For example, if you put a 3 in the first box (1A), then A1 = 3. When you are done, add up your totals. The highest total indicates your dominant Mom Mode.

| Achiever/Promote Achievement | Connector/Build Relationships | Liberator/Foster Individuality |
|---|---|---|
| 1A: | 1B: | 1C: |
| 2C: | 2B: | 2A: |
| 3A: | 3C: | 3B: |
| 4C: | 4A: | 4B: |
| 5C: | 5A: | 5B: |
| 6B: | 6A: | 6C: |
| 7B: | 7C: | 7A: |
| 8A: | 8B: | 8C: |
| Total: _____ | Total: _____ | Total: _____ |

The mode with the highest total is your preferred Mom Mode. To really hit your stride as a transformational leader, you need to operate in each of the three modes, depending on the situation, but it's helpful to know which one for you is most developed; this is the mode from which you get the most benefit, because it's where you do your best work and achieve your greatest rewards.

Typically, one mode is least developed. This is an area for personal growth. This is also the area where you may run into struggles with a co-parent, as we'll see in the pages ahead.

It's important to remember that this assessment, like any assessment, is only meant to be a starting place for opening up dialogue with your co-parent and cultivating self-knowledge.

*It is not meant to typecast you into some rigid mold that will predict your behavior in all situations.* If you pigeonhole yourself or others—"My husband is such an off-the-charts Achiever; that explains *everything*"—you are bound to obstruct your learning and limit your understanding of the complexity and capacity for change within us all.

We each operate from all three Mom Modes. Just as you will see the distinctions between each, there is also a good deal of similarity: each of the three modes relies on good relationship skills, a collaborative approach that allows for meaningful input rather than autocratic demands, and the ability to foster the child's potential.

Let's take a look at the individual Mom Modes to better understand each one.

### Achievers—Promote Achievement

> Our chief want in life is somebody who shall make us what we can be.
>
> —Ralph Waldo Emerson

Achievers' central sense of parenting satisfaction comes from their child's growth and development. They see their most important role as inspiring learning and achievement. They raise the bar high, encouraging their child to stretch, grow, and continually seek challenges. Achievers raise expectations and encourage children to reach higher levels than they would without direction. Achiever moms are at their best when driving for success. What I was struck by when talking with Achiever moms is their on-the-go lifestyles. Many described busy schedules and ambition in the context of both their work and their parenting.

Achiever mom Peggy Taylor, forty-six, a social work manager, doesn't need a lot of downtime. At work, her passion is developing staff talent. She gets a lot of satisfaction from mentoring her high-potential employees and makes a practice of instituting "stretch goals" so that people accomplish more than they initially believe they can achieve. Her best leadership moments at work come from watching her staff's self-confidence increase as they tackle new challenges.

At home, she enjoys keeping busy and fills her children's schedules with music lessons, sports teams, and language classes. "They're like sponges," she says. "I want to make sure they're exposed to as much as possible so that they flourish." Each of her kids attends a different summer camp depending on their specific interests and talents. "It's a little nutty at pickup time, but I think it's worth it if they're all doing something they love and developing skills in activities that they're good at," she says.

### Connectors—Build Relationships

> Leadership is not an affair of the head. Leadership is an affair of the heart.
>
> —Jim Kouzes and Barry Posner, *The Leadership Challenge*

Connectors' central sense of parenting satisfaction comes from emotional connection with their child. They see their most important role as nurturing and expressing affection. They strive to ensure that each family member's needs are heard and supported. Connectors build strong bonds that make children feel valued, safe, and trusted.

Connector moms feel the greatest joy when they have time to unwind and get intimate with colleagues and family members. At work, you're not likely to find the Connectors behind closed doors or in front of their computers for hours on end. They get energized by interacting with people and nurturing their relationships.

At home and at work, they can easily get irritable when they go too long without time to really connect.

Connector mom Gayle, an executive of a public relations firm with seven-year-old twin boys and a six-year-old daughter, makes a habit of having lunch with her staff to really get to know them. She is well loved and respected in her company, and when asked about her leadership philosophy, she says, "I listen to people and value what they have to say. It really starts and ends with building relationships."

At home, Gayle doesn't have a lot of time during the week to relax with her kids, so she makes the most of her weekends. She puts work aside and devotes weekend time to her family. A couple of times each year, she plans weekends with one child at a time to provide plenty of opportunities for intimate connection. "Half the fun is choosing where to go and planning our weekend trip," she says. "My son and I went to San Diego. Last summer, I took my daughter to Stinson Beach for a weekend playing in the surf."

## Liberators—Foster Individuality

> Stop shielding your children and clipping their wings. Allow your children to develop along their own lines. Don't prevent self-reliance and initiative.
>
> —Eleanor Roosevelt

Liberators' central sense of parenting satisfaction comes from seeing their children making their own choices and discovering their uniqueness. Liberators see their most important role as providing the room and the safety for their children to develop into unique, self-sufficient individuals. They strive to foster independent thinking. Liberators foster children's unique sense of self. Liberator moms hit their stride when they foster self-reliance in their children. Unlike Achiever and Connector moms, they are primarily concerned with stepping back and leaving plenty of room for their child's individuality to flourish. Liberator moms love to cultivate and honor each child's interests and choices. Rather than try to control their opinions, a Liberator mom enjoys facilitating intellectual discussions that inspire her children to formulate their own opinions.

Amy Chang, an administrative assistant for a large computer company and the mother of two teenage daughters, manages a temporary worker pool. Unlike most temp workers, people who work for Amy love their job, and many end up staying and building careers at the company. She trains them and then, as they master the job, she gives them more and more responsibility. One best moment at work she recalls was when a young woman proposed a way to streamline a laborious data inputting process. Amy made sure she got the attention of a manager who ended up giving the woman a permanent job.

At home, Amy likes to keep her children engaged in world issues and informed about problems outside their home. "Global warming, litter in our city streets, world hunger—you name it, we discuss it," says Amy. Amy encourages her kids to think about how they can contribute to the greater good in the world.

## ACQUIRING MOM MODES FROM OUR PARENTS

Where do our Mom Modes come from? Not surprisingly, we often learn them from our own mothers and fathers. Many mothers in my seminars point to their own parents as their most admired teachers and role models. Parents teach their children leadership traits by example, showing them how to be successful, build trusting relationships, and promote individuality. Our own parents have had a profound effect on the way we lead—at work or at the kitchen table. We truly do set an example that is likely to be carried out over generations.

Given that many mothers now have careers before they become parents, the workplace becomes a fertile training ground for mothering. Working mothers take the skills they cultivate at the office and bring them home. The working mothers I coach tell me that their Mom Mode plays out similarly at work and at home.

## The Achiever

Debbie, an attorney with daughters ages five and nine, was raised by a single mother with exacting standards, and she tends to lead the same way. Debbie's mother instilled strong ambition in her and her brother. "We knew my mom loved us, but she was tough," she says. Her mother expected her to do her best and pushed hard when she and her brother fell short of doing as well as she thought they could. Debbie uses this same combination of love and toughness to bring out the best in her employees and kids. Above all, she wants people to feel successful and believes that the way to accomplish that is by setting the bar high and providing opportunities for people to take risks and stretch beyond what they feel they can do. Debbie's primary goal as a parent—and a manager—is to promote success.

## The Connector

Me, I'm a Connector, as is my mom, who has an incredible gift of listening and drawing people out. When I was a kid, she seemed to possess a sixth sense of knowing what to say when I was sad or scared, and to this day, when I feel down or self-doubting, I hear my mom's words of love and encouragement.

When I managed a work team, we saw ourselves as a family. I put a premium on listening to my employees, cultivating trust, and building strong relationships. I do the same at home. I've instilled a family culture of loving relationships—my daughters adore each other (I bet Susan's kids fight all the time), we love to play games together on Sunday nights (poof—no *Sabrina*), we snuggle, and we have mock debates about who loves whom more. I can learn from my friend Susan, but I don't need to *be* her or make her choices. In fact, being her, for me and my family, would be a very bad idea. Competitions have always felt so . . . I don't know, competitive. I can't help feeling bad for all the kids who want trophies but go home empty handed, forgetting that they had a good time kicking a ball across a grassy field. Just the *thought* of spending three hours driving to and from Sacramento for a soccer game zaps my energy, not to mention sending my kid off to an unpronounceable country at age twelve.

### The Liberator

Janet's mother focused most on encouraging her children to think for themselves. She was passionate about bringing out each child's individuality and encouraging them to think for themselves. She wanted them be self-sufficient, and struggled most when they succumbed to peer pressure and surrendered their uniqueness.

"Mom would throw out a topic at the dinner table, and we were asked to share our opinion and justify it," says Janet, thirty-five, a graphic artist with a nine-year-old son. She always got the sense that her mother enjoyed it when Janet disagreed with her, especially if Janet had a strong defense for her position. At work, Janet's colleagues know that when they come to her with an idea, they'd better have a fresh, innovative perspective. At home, she's the same way: she gives her children a lot of freedom to solve their own problems and to find ways to fill their time creatively. Janet's first priority as a mom, and in her work, is to foster individuality.

## BEST MOM MOMENTS

One way to see how your Mom Mode plays out with your kids is to think about a "best mom" moment, when the fatigue of the job melts away and you feel deeply satisfied. When you

## MOM MODE QUIZ

**When your children fight, do you . . .**

- Let them go at it because sibling rivalry is fertile training ground for learning who they are? (Liberator)
- Break it up because it pains you to hear the mean voices they're using with each other? (Connector)
- Leave the room because you see it as an opportunity to strengthen their conflict resolution skills? (Achiever)

**Your son wants to play soccer. Do you . . .**

- Encourage him to join a recreational team so that he can stay with the same group of boys year after year and build a strong community of friendships? (Connector)
- Encourage him to try out for the competitive team because the coach has a strong reputation of really stretching kids to build their athletic abilities? (Achiever)
- Allow him to think about which team he is more interested in joining and why? (Liberator)

**You decide to go back to work after staying home for the first two years of your daughter's life. Do you go back to work primarily because . . .**

- You miss the adult relationships and being part of a team? You need to feel validated and respected in a way that you don't experience at home. (Connector)
- You tried to put your ambition aside for two years, but now you are excited about getting back in the game and pursuing your career goals? (Achiever)
- When you stayed home, you felt that parts of your identity started to disappear? You're eager to get back to a job that taps into a wide spectrum of your skills and interests. (Liberator)

experience a best mom moment, you know it because you feel connected with your child, you can see your positive influence, and you aren't wracked with self-doubt, wondering *Am I doing this right?*

Take a minute now to jot down some of your best mom moments. From which mode were you operating during these moments?

_____

_____

How about a best moment at work? Which mode was at play during this moment?

_____

_____

When you recognize your Mom Mode, you can really savor your best mom moments and experience them more often. You're happier and more effective when you're nourishing your Mom Mode.

## MOM MODES AND THE FIVE LEADERSHIP SKILLS

Every great leader brings the five leadership skills—motivate, focus on the big picture, empower, connect, and set an example— to life. How mothers activate each of these five behaviors differs depending on their Mom Mode. The following chart illustrates examples of how each Mom Mode expresses each of the five leadership abilities.

Now we've explored what it looks like when the best of each Mom Mode comes to life. But each mode can backfire if taken to the extreme. Let's examine the negative aspects of each mode and ways to keep your weaknesses at bay.

|  | Achiever | Connector | Liberator |
|---|---|---|---|
| Motivate | "I set the bar high because I believe in my daughter's ability to achieve even very difficult tasks." | "I give my children a lot of encouragement and praise." | "I encourage my kids to think for themselves and try to follow their lead instead of imposing my agenda on them." |
| Focus on the Big Picture | "My greatest hope is to raise my children to nurture their talents and achieve success that is meaningful to them." | "My primary goal is to raise a compassionate and kind human being." | "I want my daughter to grow up to really know who she is." |
| Empower | "I search out opportunities that challenge my kids." | "I pride myself on really knowing my daughter—when she needs my support and when I need to back off." | "I enjoy engaging my kids in debates where they have to form their own opinions." |
| Connect | "I enjoy doing projects where we are all learning together." | "I'm happiest when my son and I have heart-to-heart talks." | "It's exciting to watch my children evolve and see that they are becoming their own person." |
| Set an Example | "I have high standards for myself and expect my children to do their best and tackle big challenges." | "It's important for my kids to see that we treat our parents and friends with kindness and respect." | "I'm glad my children see me pursuing my personal ambitions." |

## MOM MODES RUN AMOK

Many a leader has failed when she ignores or takes no responsibility for her weaknesses. Just as the greatest leaders, being human, have their vulnerabilities and flaws, no mom is perfect.

Weaknesses and mistakes are as normal as breathing, but what's extraordinary are those people who are unabashedly and constantly upgrading their skills. What sets the most effective leaders apart is that the best leaders make no excuses—they have keen awareness of their weaknesses and are passionately committed to keeping them in check. Given the emotional nature of the job, given that we love our children so much that we feel overwhelmed with a yearning to "get it right," we tend to magnify our weaknesses, paying more attention to our mistakes than to our successes. The trick is to recognize and take responsibility for our weaknesses but not get so overwhelmed with self-doubt or guilt that we forget all the times we're effective.

I'm not talking about fatal flaws—dictating your child's behavior like a tyrant or making a habit of flying off the handle in a rage that can cause irreparable damage if left unchecked—but rather the run-of-the-mill imperfections that make us human. The weaknesses that accompany each mode need to be watched, but they won't endanger your child unless they get so amplified and habitual that they turn into fatal flaws.

Let's look first at the underbelly of your Mom Mode, at the weaknesses that make you lovably but not fatally flawed.

Get comfortable in your chair. Remember that you are not alone, not by a long shot. Now look over some examples illustrating common shadow sides to each Mom Mode. Recognize any? Check all that apply.

### Achievers Amok

☐ You plan a jam-packed enrichment regimen for your middle schooler to prepare her to get into an Ivy League college.

☐ You push your daughter to try out for a traveling soccer team because she shows such talent, even though she wants to stay on the recreational team with her friends.

☐ You wish your child were more like Stephanie down the street, who pulls straight A's and wins piano competitions.

☐ You worry whether your child's preschool is preparing her properly for an academic elementary school.

### Achievers may

☐ Get too caught up in their child's achievements

☐ Push their own agenda

☐ Get carried away with competition

☐ Compare their child to others

☐ Be judgmental or critical

☐ Micromanage

## Connectors Amok

☐ You talk to your daughter's teacher about a girl who is excluding your daughter at recess games, even when your daughter asked you not to.

☐ You get your child a hamster because you can't resist making her happy, even though you know full well that she will tire of it in no time and that the stinky cage will be yours to manage alone.

☐ You let your child sleep in your bed even though it costs you plenty of nights' sleep.

### Connectors may

☐ Rush in to protect or rescue

☐ Get overly involved or enmeshed in their child's emotional life

☐ Lose control of their emotions

☐ Make shortsighted decisions or accommodate unreasonable demands to avoid conflict

☐ Care too much about being liked by their children

### Liberators Amok

☐ You insist that your son "shake it off" when he whines about missing you when you leave for business trips.

☐ You snap at your child when she gets clingy in unfamiliar settings.

☐ You ridicule your teenage daughter when she tries too hard to fit in with her peers.

Liberators may

☐ Get too far removed and lose connection

☐ Feel uncomfortable when their independence is jeopardized

☐ Get impatient with neediness

☐ Lose patience with the learning process

### Quiz Analysis: Managing Your Mom Mode

Look back at your check marks. Choose an area you're committed to improving. Bypass the excuses and start right now. Leadership is all about being passionately committed to self-discovery and self-improvement. The following questions are designed to guide you through a process of discarding old habits. The questions are powerful especially if you take a bit of uninterrupted time and try not to rush through them. Some questions elicit more benefit if you ask them twice or three times in order to really drill down to the root of the problem. To assist you with the questions, I've included one mom's responses as an example. Heather, a mother of a ten-year-old daughter, participated in a Mom Mode workshop and explored how her Connector mode runs amok.

1. What Mom Mode weakness do you want to improve?

    *I get overly enmeshed in my daughter's emotional life. When she is sad, I can't disentangle from her pain. I want to fix it.*

2. What does this weakness cost you?

    *I get overly anxious and lose sleep. My daughter is starting to hide her problems from me because she gets annoyed when I get worried.*

3. What does this weakness cost your child?

    *She doesn't learn to solve her own problems. She may feel like she isn't capable of handling stressful situations when she sees how worried I get.*

4. What is the hidden benefit of this weakness? After all, there must be *some* benefit if you continue to demonstrate this behavior.

    *I feel a sense of control, like somehow my worries, my staying up fretting at night, will take away my daughter's sadness or fears.*

5. Identify a specific action you're willing to take to minimize this weakness.

    *When my daughter shares a problem with me, I will listen and resist the temptation to problem-solve.*

6. Enlist a trustworthy supporter who can help keep you on track with your new behavior. Who?

    *My husband.*

## ADJUSTING YOUR MOM MODES

Even though you have a primary Mom Mode, it's useful to be able to stretch and use the others when the situation calls for it. We all need to balance our Mom Mode with the others. A Liberator mom might err on the side of giving too much freedom, without offering the structure and guidance needed to promote success. For example, if the Liberator mom allows her child to do his homework independently when he isn't motivated to do so, or isn't able to do so, we can be sure the homework won't get done. Likewise, if an Achiever or Connector mom tips out of balance and directs her child to do her homework at a specified time and breathes down her neck until she's finished, when the child is perfectly capable of doing her homework on time and independently, this mom needlessly fosters dependence, breeds resistance, and erodes self-confidence.

Every manager struggles with determining if a performance problem is a matter of ability or motivation. Does the person lack the needed skills to get the job done, or is the problem that the person doesn't want to do the task? Whether you are at the office or with your child, different coaching strategies work best depending on the maturity, ability, and motivation of the person. For example, if your child is struggling to do his homework, is it a matter of his ability or his willingness? In other words, is the challenge a motivational one (he doesn't want to do his homework), or is the resistance related to his ability (he doesn't understand the math problems)? Diagnosing the challenge at hand helps you figure out an appropriate strategy. The next sections outline four approaches—adapted from a useful model widely used in business called Situational Leadership, developed by Paul Hersey and Ken Blanchard, and from Situational Parenting, developed by Paul Hersey—that take into account the developmental readiness of the "follower" to determine the leadership style that will work best in the situation. The most effective leaders take into account the differences between individuals and provide support that considers people's unique needs. Read the following descriptions to determine the right blend of Mom Modes that will provide the kind of support that yields the best results.

### The Direct Approach (Combining the Achiever and Connector Modes)

If your child is unmotivated and unable to do the task—let's say he can't figure out his homework alone and he'd rather do just about anything than work on his homework—you need to get in there and direct. This might mean you do one math problem, explaining each step, and then watch and provide needed assistance as the child attempts to solve the next problem on his own. Check his work and help him correct it as he goes. Don't do it for him. Unfortunately, this is not the time to go catch up on your past issues of the *New Yorker*.

### The Coach Approach (Combining the Connector and Liberator Modes)

When your child is unable to complete a task independently but is familiar with the task and motivated to do it, provide encouragement and step back. Instead of giving answers, it's better here to ask questions to inspire reflection and creative problem solving. Check her work and identify incorrect answers, encouraging her to find the correct ones. This is an opportunity for your child to experience difficulty and see that she can get through it on her own. You probably need to stay in the same room to provide support when your child asks. This isn't the best time to multitask.

### The Supportive Approach (Combining the Achiever and Liberator Modes)

If your child is able but unmotivated, it's time to set a clear limit, such as "If you get your homework done, you can go outside and play basketball before it gets dark. If you don't finish your homework, you won't get to play ball, and your teacher may keep you in for recess tomorrow." Remind your child that she is able to do the work and that you have confidence in her. Allow her to make the choice, keeping to your limit. When homework is complete, allow her to check her own work. Resist the urge to hover or nag. Enjoy the newspaper and check in from time to time.

### The Empowerment Approach (Liberator Mode)

If your child is perfectly capable as well as motivated, it's your job to allow as much independence as possible. You never want to do something for your child that he can do on his own. Allow your child to decide when to do his homework, resist reminders, and let him do it independently. Praise him for his effort and initiative and go curl up with a good book in another room.

## DAD'S MOM MODES

Just like mothers, fathers have their own personal styles of parenting. In other words, dads have Mom Modes too. They play out a little differently because fathers sometimes differ from mothers in some deep and fundamental ways. As we'll explore in more detail in the upcoming chapter about conflict, men and women often come to parenting differently.

Most moms in my workshops feel strongly that their identity is more deeply connected to their role as a parent than is the case for their male counterparts. They say they have more difficulty separating themselves from their child, carry their mom role into the office, and define themselves as mothers above all other roles. The majority of moms I speak to say they are the ones driving the carpools, arranging the play dates, buying the clothes, and making the doctor's appointments. As journalist and author Leslie Morgan Steiner writes, "I've discovered through 10 years of working motherhood the politically incorrect truth: well-educated working mothers have a far harder time juggling work and family than equivalent working fathers."

A Connector dad may struggle as Connector moms do with taking on his child's pain or rushing in to help too soon, but he may be more able to be single-minded at work than a Connector mom. Moms often tell me they worry about, even obsess about their children when they're at work, whereas their husbands go to work and, well, just work.

Although my focus here is on fathers and mothers, I also want to respect that there are all kinds of families—those with two moms, two dads, multiple moms and dads, and single parents. Regardless of their gender, when two parents operate from different modes, they can come into conflict, but they can also create just the balance that's needed.

## Complementary Modes

My husband's Liberator mode comes in handy when I'm losing my mind with worry, which, for the first year of our firstborn's life, was daily. As a Connector with overprotective tendencies, he's talked me off the parenting ledge many a time.

We enjoy reminiscing about the time we interviewed our caregiver, Chang Rong, so that I could return to work when my oldest was five months old. Chang Rong, a Chinese woman in her sixties, came with stellar credentials. She was a professional pediatric nurse in China. She was lovely and conscientious. We couldn't have found a better caregiver. The problem started when we took a walk with her to see how she interacted with our daughter, and Chang Rong handed her a flower. Anna put the flower in her mouth and bit off a petal. What if it had been poisonous? She hadn't even eaten solid food yet. Wasn't Chang Rong being careless? Yes, my reaction sounds awfully overprotective, but at the time, the situation opened a floodgate of worry about handing my daughter over to an unknown nanny.

For days after that, I sobbed at the prospect of leaving my daughter to return to work. Bad enough that I was handing Anna over to a stranger—was she incompetent to boot? It sounds crazy to me now, but night after inconsolable night, my husband had to remind me about Chang Rong's experience, her amazing references, her gentle manner, and her ability to adjust her methods to our needs and concerns—such as by not feeding Anna any random vegetation in the future. If Burke and I had both been overemotional Connectors, I don't know how any of us, Anna included, would have made it through that first year.

Our two daughters most definitely benefit from our contrasting styles. They have enjoyed climbing many a rocky peak with Daddy, laughing all the way up two-thousand-foot climbs, saying that it's a good thing Mommy stayed behind. With two parents just like me, they never—I mean never—would have jumped off that bridge in Yosemite, plunging down twelve feet into the river below, or explored that bat-filled, sinister black Subway Cave in Oregon. (I think I'm glad they did.)

## Conflicting Modes

Once we can identify where we are in sync with our co-parent, mode-wise, and where we are in disharmony, we can work the problem through more easily without getting stuck. I don't want to create the impression that getting through conflict is ever easy—but with tolerance, even appreciation, of the differences, you will still struggle but with less lingering mess. If you are able to see your partner's behavior as different from yours *and* as a helpful balance to your own attitudes and behaviors, you can co-parent with more successful results. The bottom line to keep in mind is that the greatest predictor of raising healthy kids is parents' ability to work together on behalf of their child.

Sylvie, a Connector, says her spouse complains that they haven't been away overnight since the kids were born (their oldest is six). Her husband, Peter, can't understand why she wouldn't leap at the chance of a weekend away. Sylvie felt so empty, guilty, and anxious every time they started to plan a mini vacation that they kept putting one off.

"My spouse seems uncaring," says Sylvie, a hospital administrator. "He thinks I merge with our son, Noah, blurring our boundaries." During a workshop discussion about Mom Modes,

Sylvie admitted that her Liberator husband's better sense of boundaries between himself and their child was helpful and that when she let him, he balanced out her overreactive leanings. The balance, she conceded, would provide a healthier environment for their son.

Lindsay, a Liberator mom who works in a university hospital part-time, struggled with her Connector husband until she recognized that they used complementary styles—and that this benefited her kids. She spent five years arguing with her husband about how to get the kids to bed. After a day at home with her three children, ranging from three to seven years old, she longed for time to read and talk with her husband. The problem came when her husband stretched out the bedtime ritual and got the kids to sleep later and later. Lindsay worried that her husband's tactics were making it impossible for the children to fall asleep by themselves. After taking the Mom Mode assessment, she had a different view.

"Now I can recognize that my husband, a Connector, and I have a style difference. I probably married him because he is so comfortable reaching out and connecting with others where I'm more likely to get reclusive." She began to see the situation beyond "I'm right, you're wrong."

## When Conflicts Hit an Impasse

Sometimes when two parents have different modes, they balance each other out. But other times, conflicts aren't resolved—instead, they escalate. For example, Ann, an Achiever, believes that her children need to build talents from an early age or will face unnecessary obstacles to a bright future. Her spouse, Jorge, a Connector, thinks she's over the top with worry about their kids' future success when they're only in elementary school. Their modes play out in opposite extremes, and they can't find their way to a compromise. Ultimately, one person gives in but feels resentful. Their conflict reached the boiling point when

Ann wanted to put the kids in a Spanish immersion program five days a week for six weeks of the summer. Jorge thinks summers should be fun and that Ann was ruining their childhood.

The challenge is to repeatedly ask what is most important to support the child's needs. Once you're engaged in a power struggle, it may become more important to win the argument, losing sight of what's best for the child. Working together as a team provides the healthy base every child needs to succeed, but there are times when the messiness of dueling values makes it hard to stay united.

Melanie, a recently divorced graphic artist, is dead set against homework. She helps her daughter finish it, but only the minimum and never with her heart in it. Kids need downtime when they come home from school, she says, and homework has little added value. Melanie's ex-husband, Mitch, an Achiever, feels that more homework, not less, is needed. He thinks that his daughter is getting lazy and isn't learning responsibility, let alone her multiplication facts. She needs more drills and more structure. Melanie's Connector mode kicks into overdrive—she can use the homework battle as a way to connect with her child and compete with her ex-husband for the title of the favorite parent. Mitch's worry about his daughter's academic success throws his mode into overdrive, and the two become increasingly polarized, unable to find a happy middle ground.

The way back, as we will explore in the next chapter and in Leadership Strategy 5, is to remember that you and your co-parent are a team with a unifying purpose: to work together to support your child's best interests. If you can respect the other's tactics, knowing that you're each doing what you feel is best for your child, you can reduce the frequency and heat of your conflicts, avoid putting your child in the position of having to choose sides, and yield the added benefit of modeling cooperation. Each Mom Mode can turn destructive if parents aren't willing to examine their motives and stay focused on the big picture—what is best for their child.

## Same Modes

When co-parents have the same mode, there may be fewer conflicts, but there are dangers to watch out for.

For example, overinvolvement can be a hazard when both parents are Connectors. Diane Ehrensaft, child psychologist and author of *Parenting Together,* describes the dangers of what she calls "wall-to-wall parenting," a phenomenon in which, with good intentions, two parents "overparent," leaving a child feeling emotionally suffocated and unable to rely on her resources to assist herself.

Physicians Pam and Daniel, forty and forty-one, are both Achievers. There is no question in their family that school comes first. They are disciplined about homework and send their children to schools known for their academic rigor.

"When the kids were young, we fretted about finding the right preschool, played Mozart to foster math aptitude, the works. We were over the top," says Pam.

They've toned it down since, but they can still get overanxious about their kids' success. Because they're so similar in their approach, they don't have anyone telling them to ease up. This can create problems for kids who already confront the perils of a pressure-filled existence.

Same-mode couples can more easily lose perspective than couples who possess complementary modes. Therefore, these parents will benefit from regularly reviewing the typical ways their mode runs amok and taking the Mom Mode Quiz earlier in this chapter to commit to actions that keep weaknesses in check.

□ □ □

Knowing your leadership style is an important way to begin to build self-awareness, a critical factor contributing to leaders' effectiveness. But that's not all you'll need when you confront conflict. You'll also benefit from an easy-to-use, step-by-step process that minimizes the defensiveness and anger that often flare up with conflict. Conflicts can wreak havoc, pulling you away from your big-picture goals and triggering your vulnerabilities. In the next chapter, we'll see how you can avoid common mistakes that turn conflicts into recurring power struggles. You'll learn effective approaches to handling conflicts in every area of your life.

# LEADERSHIP STRATEGY 3

# *Managing Conflict*

Once the realization is accepted that even between the closest human beings infinite distances continue to exist, a wonderful living side by side can grow up, if they succeed in loving the distance between them which makes it possible for each to see the other whole against the sky.
—Rainer Maria Rilke, in *Letters to a Young Poet*

Faye Wong, the owner and founder of a small import business and the mother of Christina, age twelve, used to feel so overwhelmed by pressure on the job that she ended up screaming at everyone.

"A lot of people felt I was an angry person—and I guess I was," says Faye. Given her high employee turnover and low morale, she realized it was time to take stock of her behavior and make some changes.

When she looked at the results of her behavior, it was clear that what she was doing wasn't working: people either became quiet and compliant, doing the bare minimum and staying off Faye's radar, or they pushed back like teenagers, became defensive, and rebelled. Either way, she wasn't getting the collaboration she needed to keep her business afloat.

The times she was most effective at work, Faye realized, were when she wasn't able to lash out at people directly. Because many of her employees were overseas and in a different time zone, she often couldn't pick up the phone and yell at them when something went wrong. Instead she wrote e-mails, pushing the "send later" button. The next morning after she calmed down, she usually discovered that the e-mail message would have caused more harm than good, so she deleted the messages and tried to work out a solution to the problem more calmly.

Faye realized that her "send later" strategy may have saved her business, so she started using that response more consciously. Her gut reaction is still to go straight to yelling, but now she has a mechanism to regulate herself, which is an essential characteristic of good leadership. Her new anger-regulating strategy became self-reinforcing: emboldened by higher productivity and morale, she was happier, and her employees were more invested in working hard to solve problems.

Faye wished relations at home would improve as well. But with a hands-off husband, a full-time job, and a preteen who wasn't getting her schoolwork done and was, more often than not, tuning her out when she tried to help, Faye found her household in constant turmoil. After an exhausting day of handling one work crisis after another without blowing her fuse, Faye would come home to find her daughter's homework planner in disarray, and explode.

But Faye knew that if she could turn her company around, she could turn her family life around, too. She decided to try the same strategy: instead of reacting in real time, she would press an imaginary "send later" button. If she didn't have the different time zone built in to give her the delayed response that worked so effectively at her job, she would have to create her own time zone in which she could "delete" her reaction and come back to her daughter with a sense of calm. So when she felt her anger rising, she left the room, emptied the dishwasher, or read a book.

Just as at work, Faye's strategy for managing her anger improved the situation at home too. When she was more relaxed, she found that she and her daughter could work together on ways to organize her school calendar, and they began to have fun putting their heads together about school projects. The struggles didn't evaporate, but they lessened, and best of all, the connection between Faye and Christina strengthened. Faye gradually recognized that her anger stemmed from a fear that her business and her daughter's success were in jeopardy. Understanding what was underneath her outbursts allowed her to look at the events that set off her emotions and to recognize the impact of her behavior—if her anger broke her connection with her daughter, she would only hurt her opportunity to influence her daughter's success. Faye also recognized that her interpretation of the events that triggered big emotions was flawed. For example, Christina's disorganized backpack didn't mean she would fail in school.

Four primary coping strategies were critical to Faye's ability to keep her anger in check: she used her time-out strategy to regain perspective and a sense of calm; she gained a better understanding of the events that prompted her anger; she realized the negative impact of her anger, so she could be more sympathetic and less blaming; and she challenged her faulty interpretations of the situations that set off her anger and fear.

## PREVENTING CONFLICT IN THE FIRST PLACE

Like Faye, we all lose our cool at times. Inevitably, the simultaneous acts of working and running a family will fill your life with conflict. A mother losing her temper is common in kitchens across America. If communicating effectively during conflict is a true test of leadership, I suppose I failed dismally when my nine-year-old pitched an explosive fit about going out to dinner, and my response was to scream, "Fine, you stay home . . . alone!" and pretended to leave the house.

In a workshop one morning, Marian J. shared this: "About three years ago when my daughter was five, she said, 'I hate you, Mom.' Without thinking, I heard myself reply, 'I hate you, too.'

I felt awful the minute I said it. I still feel awful, three years later!"

Sally W. chimed in: "I announced to my husband and my son, ten, and daughter, fifteen: 'I've had it with all of you. I'm off duty. I'm going on strike until further notice.' Then I stomped up to my bedroom and slammed the door."

We've all had those moments, and those days. The key is to see them as opportunities for building your skills at managing conflict. If you practice good communication skills, you can prevent conflicts from occurring in the first place. The problem is that as obvious as the essentials of good interpersonal skills are, they can elude you when your emotions get triggered. Even though we know what to do to maintain health—exercise and eat right—we aren't necessarily out jogging every morning instead of eating croissants. So I'm going to remind you of several crucial strategies that you can use yourself and model for your children to keep conflict to a minimum. But even the happiest families and most productive workplaces have conflict, so we will go through a powerful six-step process to resolve any conflict.

## FOUR BUILDING BLOCKS OF EFFECTIVE COMMUNICATION

Before we dive in with practical tools to mitigate a bad mood, here's the best tip of all: forget about getting it all right. Conflict is a messy business, and becoming an exemplary leader is hard enough. You don't need the guilt and self-loathing when you mess up and let "Shut up!" slip out of your mouth. Give yourself a break, take responsibility for maturing as a parent and leader, and if you feel you've messed up, look at it as an opportunity to learn some lessons that will help you avoid future mistakes.

The four building blocks of effective communication are

1. Keeping perspective, keeping your cool
2. Building listening skills

3. Saying what you mean

4. Avoiding lecturing, judging, and attacking

## Keeping Perspective, Keeping Your Cool

In corporations, great leaders are the ones who can step back and see the forest for the trees. At home, that's often harder to do. How do leaders manage to step back and keep their cool?

One way—as Faye realized—is to learn to push your pause button. When you feel a blowup coming on, use that early warning system to pause, step out of the action, and regain perspective. In my classes, I call this "engaging brain before mouth." When I helped the management team at a psychiatric hospital, they called it getting out of the "emotional mind." Whatever you call it, you can engage that highly evolved mommy brain by knowing in advance the kinds of situations that cause you to lose your temper.

For me, I am set off when I get home from an evening board meeting to find that our kids haven't taken showers and my husband hasn't managed to get up from the TV. "It's a really good match. Mexico's ahead," he says to me cheerfully—and cluelessly—as I enter the room, ready to launch into my tirade. I tell myself to resist the urge to react. Pause, take a breath, leave the room, or count to ten. Open your mind to more positive possibilities—your husband and daughter had great bonding time watching their favorite soccer teams together. They even cleaned the kitchen before they settled into watching sports. Given a little time, your anger will subside and your perspective will expand so that you can respond more effectively. Force a break in the action, and gradually the behavior that's driving you mad ceases to rile you. This takes practice!

In my workshops, I hear lots of great ideas from parents about how to avoid blowing a fuse. Every tactic has the same thing in common: putting on the brakes instead of speeding mindlessly into a communication collision.

One mom copes with her child's hostile outbursts by taking a moment in her bedroom to scream into a pillow. Another pretends that she's on reality TV, and millions of people are observing what she'll do next. Another breathes and says to herself, "This won't seem so bad tomorrow." And still another mom tries to figure out what the feelings are behind the content of the words thrown at her.

The bottom line is that we will continue to overreact occasionally—the job is too intense to stay calm in every situation. For most of us, it is nearly impossible to nail the right tone and words when we're trying to find matching socks, fix waffles, make seventeen pigtails for Wacky Hair Day, and get the kids to school on time. But if we can minimize those times we melt down, we not only feel better about ourselves but also open up communication by providing a safe place for our kids to express their full range of emotions.

If you're developing the urge to scream, take a breather. After you've regained your composure, set a clear goal for yourself.

An executive director I coached for many years complained that her staff thought she was moody. I asked her to describe one behavior she would like to commit to using when under pressure. Her goal: use a calm voice. By simply focusing on one behavior, she was able to measure her progress and hold herself accountable to a new habit. After just one week, her staff noticed the difference and felt the tension in the office lift.

Ask yourself, What can I do differently to keep the pressure down? For example, do you need a peaceful transition period with just you and your newspaper when you get home from work? If so, you have to enlist your kids and spouse. With a clear agreement, you get to read the paper, and you won't spend the first half hour after coming home from work snapping at your kids. Hop in the driver's seat and ask for what you need.

I don't have to tell you that you are constantly being watched and mimicked by your children. If you have employees reporting to you, they are watching your every move too. Maturing as a leader at work and at home means learning to step back and recognize your reactions *and their impact on others.*

One of my favorite bosses once said, "When we hit difficult times, I know that everyone watches my reaction. If I'm optimistic and calm, others follow suit. If I bring my tension into the office, I can watch it spread throughout the department. What helps me is to remember I'm there to keep my eye on our ultimate goals and navigate us through rough waters. When I get off course, my staff gets off course."

The same is true at home. You set the tone. I'm reminded of my fear of flying, an anxiety I acquired with motherhood. When we hit turbulence, I immediately look at the flight attendants. If they remain calm, I breathe a sigh of relief.

You won't always exhibit ideal leadership behavior. Did you miss the mark? Skip the guilt, recommit to your intention to model good Mom-in-Chief leadership, and try again. The important thing is to remember that you set the example. You're modeling behavior for others to imitate.

If you don't get it right the first time, you can start over and try again. Elaine Fukuhara Schilling, a management trainer and mother of James, fourteen, came home after a long day at work. She opened the door to find her son playing video games, surrounded by the mess she had asked him to clean up that morning.

Furious, she yelled, "James, I asked you to clean up your mess!"

"Hi Mom, nice to see you too," James replied.

Elaine simply closed the door, stood behind it for a moment, and reopened it.

"Hi James, how was your day?"

"Hi Mom. I had a good day. I guess I need to clean up my mess now, right?"

"Yep, that's right," she said.

Elaine realized how important it was to stay focused on the bigger picture: that her most valued goal is to have a close relationship with her son. With her big-picture goal in sight, she had the wherewithal to correct her behavior and achieve a better result.

## Building Listening Skills

The second critical communication skill is the most difficult: listening—really listening. The keys to true listening: curiosity and good questions. Listening often needs a good push to head the conversation in the right direction. "How was your day?" doesn't cut it.

One of the best listeners I know, Karl, an executive of a biotech firm, walked into his Tuesday morning management meeting and, instead of hearing the usual cheerful greetings, found everyone silent, arms crossed. When he said good morning, all he got was grunts. Next he said, "Is there something going on I should know about?" Still nothing except from one person who offered that he needed to get back to the lab to finish an important project. Karl looked at me with a confused expression on his face. Then he looked back at the group and said, "I can see you're upset about something. Is there someone who wants to fill me in?" Still nothing.

Karl could have gone around the group asking each person for a status report on the project that they had all been working on for the past month, but he had a hunch that he needed to bring to the surface what might be making everyone look so glum. He took a stab and asked, "Is the announcement about moving the West research crew to our Zurich office part of what's got people upset this morning?" Two people spoke at once, airing their concerns about breaking up the team that had worked so well together for more than a year. Once the problem was out on the table, Karl's job was to listen, acknowledge the feelings in the room, and validate their concerns before he did any talking himself. Karl was an adept enough leader to know

instinctively that he had to listen carefully, showing he understood the concerns and respected his managers' views.

"I knew the decision had already been made without their
input, and they had every right to feel bitter about being
excluded and upset about their team dismantling. I couldn't
reverse the decision or make excuses about it, but I could listen and validate their emotions," said Karl. After listening for a
good half hour and reflecting back what people said to make sure
he understood their concerns, he explained the company's rationale for the unilateral decision and acknowledged the unfortunate consequences to his work team. Although the group wasn't
happy, they expressed appreciation for Karl's willingness to hear
them out and acknowledge their concerns.

With children who seem reluctant to talk, the challenge is
similar to Karl's. As a good leader, you need to read the cues and
ask good questions: "You look upset. Did something upsetting happen at school today that you'd like to tell me about?" But many
mothers have another kind of challenge. Let's face it: we find it
hard after a long day to listen to our child chatter on and on about
a princess and her pink unicorn pet or the ins and outs of wall ball
and how Wesley always breaks the rules and does cherry bombs
when cherry bombs are definitely against the rules, but he lies and
says he did a waterfall, not a cherry bomb, but everyone in line
saw him do a cherry bomb . . . You get the picture.

The solution is twofold: be honest when you aren't able to
listen and then carve out a specific time when you can settle in
with your child and really pay attention. The power of truly listening has tremendous benefits for cultivating a strong connection with your child.

It's interesting to observe yourself. How much time do you
really think you're listening to your child versus tuning out?
I once conducted this eye-opening experiment during a day trip
to the beautiful Point. Reyes coast of Northern California. As
we drove up the winding, redwood-lined highway, I kept track

of each time my mind wandered away as my two daughters were speaking to me.

I had fancied myself a better-than-average listener. But I was startled to find that I spent a good deal of time "pretend listening" as I thought of other "more pressing" concerns, such as what I would make for dinner when all we had in the refrigerator was three kinds of mustard, and what was the name of that Judi Dench movie about Queen Victoria that I liked so much? I had become painfully accomplished at nodding at the right time and saying "uh huh" so that I got away with not listening (or at least I thought I did).

Try the same experiment. How much do you truly listen? Are you aware when your mind slips away? How does your sense of connection change when you are really listening? When your emotions are set off, what would the results be if you listened with curiosity and patience instead of overreacting?

What I've found over the years is that the best leaders really *want* to listen. They are able to set aside their emotions and put themselves in someone else's shoes. Simply put, they are truly interested in understanding the feelings of another human being. If you watch good leaders, you will discover that they listen with their ears and eyes. They are curious about the feelings behind the words and what larger issues are at play. They listen for tone and watch for body language. They listen to the "music" behind the words to get clues to the real issue at hand. They are more concerned with understanding what is being said than formulating their response. Perhaps most important, they don't let their own feelings get in the way of their listening and understanding.

Being a good listener takes practice. Try listening to your child, your coworker, or your husband with one simple goal: listen for a full minute or two without letting your mind wander. How many distracting thoughts wandered into your mind? Take a little time each day to pay attention to where your mind goes as you listen to others. When you wander off, bring your attention back.

Keep the following tips in mind to improve the quality of your listening:

- Nod and make eye contact to demonstrate you are paying attention.
- Listen for emotions and respectfully acknowledge them. What are the feelings behind the words? Is the person angry, sad, worried? If you're not sure, check it out. Say, "It sounds like you're sad about your teacher going on maternity leave. I'd be sad too. I wonder if you're worried about what your substitute teacher will be like."
- Don't interrupt or finish the other person's sentence.
- When you are busy, don't pretend to listen. Say, "I can't listen right now, but when I finish with my phone call, I'll give you my full attention."
- Ask open-ended questions that move the conversation forward. For example, say, "Who else did the science project with you?" "How did you feel after the performance?" "What was most fun about your day?" "Why did the teacher ask the class to stay inside for recess?" "What did you like best about the field trip?"
- Make time to get away from home and have a date night with your spouse. You will find it's much easier to listen to your partner when your child isn't interrupting your every sentence.

Listening fully without getting distracted or overreacting takes discipline, but it's well worth the effort. When parents become master listeners, they not only show their children respect and build connection but also teach an invaluable interpersonal skill that escapes most adults.

## Saying What You Mean

Once you're a master listener, you're ready to speak with the added bonus of being heard. I often feel like a character in a *Far*

*Side* cartoon. Remember the one where the woman says to her dog, "You stay off the furniture, Ginger, or else! You hear me, Ginger? . . ."? What the dog hears, shown in a separate panel, is "Blah blah blah GINGER blah blah GINGER . . ." It's very funny, but also an excellent example of how communication and efforts to resolve conflicts can fail.

Countless parents tell me during workshops that they are amazed at the capacity of their children to tune them out. As one mom explained, "First time I make a request, it's a throwaway. Second time, again, optional. Third time, I yell, they look up, wide-eyed, and they listen." The entire room broke out in nods and laughter.

The same thing happens at work. The boss makes speech after speech about how things are going to change around here, but soon employees tune out, having learned that nothing really changes; and when new initiatives are introduced, they soon fizzle out, teaching people not to pay serious attention.

The third building block to good communication is to say what you mean. The big mistake that some leaders make, which instantly undermines their credibility, is to fail to align what they *say* with what they *do*. My nine-year-old explains this phenomenon well. She said to me, "Mom, why do grown-ups say 'We're leaving' and then talk and talk instead of leaving?" Good question, simple answer: we are in the habit of not saying what we mean. When we don't say what we mean, we teach people to tune us out.

Ask yourself, Am I prepared to back up what I say with action? If you aren't really ready to leave the play date, hold off on telling your child it's time to go.

Let's look at ways you can avoid conflict and increase the chances of getting a positive response when you ask your child to do something. Suppose your child engages in power struggles with you each morning. You wish she would get her shoes on and brush her teeth without your asking over and over and finally exploding. Keeping your big-picture goal in mind, you need to say what you mean. If your big-picture goal is to instill responsibility and respect in your child, you recognize that your communication has to be backed up with action. Here are some tips to increase your chances of being heard and getting the results you want:

1. Calmly but firmly make it clear that her resistance frustrates you, without belittling or criticizing. "When you don't get your shoes on when I ask you to, I feel angry and frustrated."

2. Find a time when you're not rushed and you're alone with your child. Establish a specific game plan. State your "nonnegotiable." "I'm going to ask you once to put on your shoes." At first, provide hands-on guidance. This is a time for shared responsibility. Once her new behavior sticks (wait at least one week), you can leave more room for her to get her shoes on independently.

3. Back your message with action. Have some fun jointly deciding on consequences and rewards. Celebrate small successes. "If you get your shoes on after I ask once every day this week, we'll think about something fun we can do together this weekend."

4. Make sure that what you're asking for is achievable. As needed, divide up the request into smaller parts. Move to toothbrushing only after the shoe behavior improves.

5. Make the consequences clear. "If you don't get your shoes on after one request, we will get to school late. Your teacher doesn't like it when you come in late because it disrupts the class." Or "When we're running late, we have to run to school, which I know you don't like to do. If you get ready when I ask, we get to have more fun stopping and looking into store windows along the way."

You've shown you mean business when you make a reasonable request and follow it up with consequences. By saying what you mean, you avoid a lot of needless headaches and flared tempers.

## Avoiding Lecturing, Judging, and Attacking

The fourth building block for effective communication is to avoid behavior that shuts communication down or, worse, hurts people. The more we avoid what I call junk communication, the more you'll find you avoid conflict and get a better response. Junk communication is like junk mail—you find it annoying and you throw it away. When you're tempted to engage in junk communication, you may as well save your voice. No one's listening. There are several typical junk communications: lecturing, judging, and attacking.

### Lecturing

You know you're lecturing when you hear yourself start a monologue with something like

"Here is the way to do it."
"You should do it this way."
"It would be better if you . . ."
"You're old enough to know . . ."
"You need to go apologize. You should have known better."

A typical lecture goes on long after the point is made. If you're trying to address undesirable behavior, the less said, the better. It's important to keep in mind that lectures often contain judgmental language and overjustifications.

### Judging

A close cousin of lecturing is judging. It's amazing how many times I hear bosses point out undesired behavior using judgmental language—for example, "Your work is careless." The employee is left wondering what, specifically, about her work is careless. Using judgmental language, you're guaranteed to get a defensive reaction. Besides that, the employee doesn't know what to do to remedy the problem. If instead the boss says, "Your budget contains three errors," points them out, and asks the person to correct them by Wednesday, the employee knows exactly what needs correcting and doesn't feel degraded.

Here's a helpful formula to keep in mind when correcting behavior: (1) state the behavior; (2) make a request; and (3) define the impact of the behavior you're correcting, without judging. For example:

**Behavior:** "You've been on the computer for thirty minutes."

**Request:** "Please turn off your computer now and do your homework."

**Impact:** "If you wait any longer, you'll be up too late and won't have time to read your book."

Notice how the behavior is defined, without judging; the request is direct, respectful, and brief; and the impact is clear.

Here's another example:

**Behavior:** "Next time you do a cooking project, you need to clean up without my asking."

**Request:** "Please come in and clean up now."

**Impact:** "I'm less likely to say yes next time you ask to do a cooking project unless you clean up without my having to remind you."

You know you're in judgment mode if you hear yourself say

"What a foolish thing to do."

"You are way too old to behave like that."

"You're being rude."

Judgmental words not only trigger defensiveness but also fail to explain the undesirable behavior so that the child understands how it can be corrected. To avoid conflict and defensiveness, replace judgmental words with specific statements about behavior you can *see* or *hear*.

### Attacking

Related to lecturing except that it happens in a flash, "drive-by communication" is a personal attack that you usually make as you're rushing from one thing to another. It comes out of nowhere and catches people off guard. For example, on a mad rush through the living room, you notice that your kids are eating crackers that are crumbling all over the couch, and you yell, "Look at what you're doing. I am sick and tired of cleaning up after you slobs. You know better than to eat on the couch." Like lecturing, attacks are packed with judging and derision. If it's important enough to say, take the time to say it, but minus the judgmental language: "Please stop eating on the couch, and clean up the crackers." After you make your request, you can add the impact: "When you eat on the couch, it gets stained and it's difficult to clean."

## CONFLICT RESOLUTION STEP-BY-STEP

Think about a person at work who brings out your worst behavior—that person with whom you are in constant conflict. I'm guessing that you feel that this person doesn't respect your feelings, doesn't listen well, and sees you as the problem. You've tried to get this person to see the situation from your perspective, to no avail. Now you're convinced that the other person does things just to infuriate you.

For instance, Victor, a manager, signed up for a professional conference that he had attended the previous year. When Victor's boss, Anita, told him he couldn't go, he was furious. He stormed into Anita's office to complain. Anita told Victor she had made it crystal clear that his request for conferences had to go through her because their professional development budgets had been cut in half that year. As Anita saw it, Victor was acting in his usual Lone Ranger manner, taking care of his needs without considering the larger group or the importance of cost containment. Victor, on the other hand, was sick and tired of feeling micromanaged by Anita. He felt that she had it out for him and enjoyed wielding power over him.

There were classic ingredients in Victor and Anita's story that kept the conflict in gridlock: neither saw his or her part in the conflict, both blamed the other for their conflicts, they couldn't see any merit to the other's behavior, and they were unaware of any common ground between them.

Believe it or not, Victor and Anita emerged from this conflict and gradually built a healthy work relationship. How? Once they both saw that they ultimately wanted the same thing—to achieve the same work goals and to have a respectful relationship—they decided that collaborating was far preferable to having clenched fists every time they passed each other in the hallways. By going through a step-by-step conflict resolution process (which I describe in the next section), they each admitted their part in the conflicts between them. That was a gigantic turning point. Their acknowledgment of their role freed them up from the vicious cycle of justifying their own point of view and pointing fingers of blame at each other. They began to listen openly and understand the other's feelings and eventually appreciate the good intentions both had to meet their common goals. Anita consented to Victor's attending his conference with Victor's word that he would get approval for conferences in the future. With concrete agreements in place, and a willingness to shift from blaming each other to assuming responsibility, trust between them steadily grew.

When I worked with Victor and Anita, I guided them through a six-step process that helped them see their common ground, empathize, and shift away from a win-lose mindset.

When I started helping mothers deal with conflicts in their families, I noticed that the process I used in the business world works equally well at home. With very young children, you'll need to modify the process a little, but let's start by looking at each of the steps and how they worked in a conflict between a mom and her eight-year-old daughter.

## RESOLVING POWER STRUGGLES WITH CHILDREN

The conflicts that plague parents most are power struggles. I hear about the parent-child tugs-of-war, those battles in which that forty-pound person debates you on the merits of not bathing, until you finally give in. "How can this little person, thirty-plus years my junior, have so much power over me? He runs the show!" says one mom.

Here's a conflict you can probably relate to. A mom comes to pick up her son from a play date. She says to him, "Nate, we're leaving now." He promptly replies, "No. You're not the boss of me. We're not leaving." She smiles politely at the hosting mom, lamely explaining, "He hates to say good-bye."

After chatting mindlessly with the host for five minutes, the mom tries again. "Hey, buddy, we need to go pick up your sister. Let's go, sweetie." Fast-forward ten more minutes. She says they need to go, for the umpteenth time. Nate is clearly winning the contest, and the mom is feeling embarrassed and defeated. Her temper is rising. She erupts, carrying a kicking and screaming Nate out the front door, yelling, "Stop it now or else you will *never* have a play date again!"

When a mom snaps into punitive mode, the child learns that conflicts are resolved with one person winning and one losing. We won't prevent every battle, but children can learn important lessons about respect and empathy when we handle conflicts effectively. In the situation with Nate, the mom can validate her son's feelings by saying, "You sound really angry," defusing the conflict. She can take ownership for losing her temper and for lingering after saying it was time to leave, thus showing a willingness to look at how she contributed to the conflict. At the same time, she can establish clear expectations that get them to a win-win solution: "We both like going to Jack's house. If that's going to happen, we need to make some agreements about what needs to happen when it's time to leave."

In a nutshell, resolving conflict with children boils down to respectful listening, validating feelings, sharing responsibility, and getting to win-win solutions. Keeping these elements in mind can help you resolve conflict with kids in less time and with less lingering mess; best of all, you can strengthen your relationships.

Here's an example of another power struggle and a discussion of what went wrong and how the conflict could have been handled more effectively.

Darlene, the mother of Kiley, eight years old, was preparing a Christmas dinner when her eighty-year-old mother called on the telephone. After talking to her for several minutes, Darlene asked her daughter, who was busy building a Lego tower, to say hello to her grandmother. Kiley ignored her mother's requests. Darlene handed her daughter the phone and whispered, "Just tell her you love her or wish her a Merry Christmas." Kiley pushed the phone away. Darlene shoved the phone back in Kiley's hand and gave her a stern look. When she finally took the phone, Kiley put it to her ear, said "Bye," and hung up. Darlene was furious, wondering how her daughter could be so insensitive. Kiley ran away in tears. Darlene's husband, who had his own share of conflict with his mother-in-law, couldn't resist putting in his two cents: "Can I hang up on your mother next time she calls?"

"Not funny," Darlene snapped back.

Let's examine and resolve this conflict.

## Step One: Identifying the Ideal Outcome

Remember big-picture parenting? Before rushing into any conflict, keep focused on your highest priority. In this case, Darlene wanted to instill respect in her daughter. This meant she had two tasks before her: to deal with the conflict at hand, making clear how she expected Kiley to treat her grandmother, and to teach respect. But she knew that to teach respect, she needed to treat Kiley respectfully, even though she was furious.

Things get more complicated when your co-parent has a different desired outcome. For example, Darlene's husband wanted Kiley to be able to act authentically and assert her needs, yet once they sat down and discussed the situation, he agreed that respectful behavior was his primary goal as well.

## Step Two: Listening to Each Other

Darlene went up to Kiley's room and sat on her bed. After a while, Kiley was ready to talk. She said, "I don't like talking on the phone. And Grandma always asks me lots of questions that I don't want to answer." Darlene says she realized that she had asked her daughter to do something that made Kiley feel uncomfortable. Instead of jumping to a solution, she just listened.

## Step Three: Expressing Feelings

Scratch the surface of any conflict, and you will find a complicated mix of emotions. Even this relatively small conflict was supercharged with emotion. Until feelings are understood and acknowledged, the conflict is unlikely to be resolved.

Darlene explained to Kiley that she felt sad that Kiley's grandmother lives so far away and doesn't know her granddaughter that well. She also told her daughter she felt frustrated that Kiley didn't want to talk to her grandmother on the phone.

"I had strong feelings about my husband and my mother's history of mild animosity. What I felt but didn't share with Kiley was that I worried that they'd never have the chance to form a loving relationship," said Darlene.

There are a lot of complicated emotions Kiley unwittingly ran into. After Darlene calmed down, she realized that Kiley is only eight and hasn't had much experience speaking on the phone, let alone talking to her grandmother, whom she has met only a handful of times. Her husband later shared with Darlene that he thought she was coming down too hard on Kiley, as she hardly knows her grandmother and phone conversations can be awkward.

### Step Four: Sharing Responsibility

When you're in conflict with a child, it is your job as a parent to let go of proving you're right and instead to acknowledge how you contributed to the conflict. How did Darlene play into this conflict? She didn't make her expectations about talking on the phone clear ahead of time. She lost her temper. "I know I let my own complicated feelings of guilt about living so far away from my mother and tension about my husband not appreciating my mother influence the situation," said Darlene.

If you can let go of justifying that you're right and the other person is wrong, you're well on your way to living with less conflict. In every conflict I've ever mediated, the impasse remains until one person shifts away from the right-wrong mindset.

### Step Five: Committing to Action

Darlene planned to establish clear expectations about phone manners that both she and her daughter could accept. Darlene resolved to use this situation to express her emotions and help her daughter express hers.

### Step Six: Appreciating Each Other

We all know it's hard to stay calm, especially when your own mother is horrified by your child's poor manners. When you feel your patience wearing thin, it's a good time to pause, step back, and take stock of the situation from a broader perspective. Darlene, once she stopped to reflect on why the situation provoked her anger, was able to validate her daughter's upset feelings and reconnect. We'll learn more about the importance of practicing appreciation on a regular basis in the next chapter.

## TEACHING CONFLICT RESOLUTION TO OLDER CHILDREN

When children are in middle school, they're old enough to learn how to manage their own conflicts. I took a shot at facilitating a conflict between my daughter and her friend in order to teach them the six-step conflict resolution process.

It wasn't the first time Gwen and my daughter, Anna, had tussled. Friends for half their lives, the girls, then twelve, often butted heads over matters big and small. Each conflict had distinct details, but the headline remained the same.

Gwen, in Anna's view, was too sensitive. Anna, in Gwen's view, was too pushy. Yet they were close, loyal friends who somehow managed to get through their conflicts. Unfortunately, the resentments lingered so long between arguments that they sometimes wondered if their friendship would survive.

So when Anna came home complaining of yet another incident with Gwen, I decided I would put my leadership consultant hat on and facilitate their conflict. Anna was annoyed with Gwen for, in her mind, wasting precious recess time arguing over the rules of basketball when they could've been playing. She admitted that she got too frustrated with Gwen and had probably hurt her feelings.

The next afternoon when Gwen came home from school with Anna, I asked if they were game to try an approach to conflict that I used in my work with organizations. They shrugged their shoulders, and both uttered a barely audible "OK." I led the girls into the living room and whipped out my flipchart and markers. After setting some ground rules with them including listening to each other and not criticizing, we were ready to begin.

## Step One: Identifying the Ideal Outcome

The first step is to figure out what each person sees as an ideal outcome. This is important because during a conflict it's easy to focus only on the differing points of view, losing sight of areas of agreement.

> **Jamie:** Let's start by figuring out what you both see as an ideal outcome of this talk. In other words, what do you hope will happen?
>
> **Gwen:** I don't want our friendship to be hurt. I want to know that our friendship is strong even if we argue.
>
> **Anna:** Me either. I mean, I don't want our friendship to end.
>
> **Jamie:** Great. So you both have the same goal. If I were to put it in a positive way, your goal is this: you both want your friendship to continue and be strong. Is this correct?

They both nodded, looking straight at me.

I added what I knew to be true: "I know you care about each other and value each other's friendship." They looked at each other, nodded, and smiled.

## Step Two: Listening to Each Other

Conflicts can't be resolved until people listen to each other's point of view. Most conflicts cause people to dig in their heels and close down to new ways of seeing the situation. Energy is spent on justifying blame. Step two helps the people in conflict better understand the other's view of the situation.

**Jamie:** Now you will each get a chance to briefly explain how you
see the situation. Who would like to go first?

**Gwen:** I didn't like it when Anna yelled at me about the rules
of the basketball game we were playing at recess. And
then I *really* didn't like it when Anna shoved me away
from the ball.

**Jamie:** Thanks, Gwen. Anna?

**Anna:** *(after half a minute of silence)* Um, well, I get really frustrated when the rules keep changing, because then we spend
the whole recess talking about the rules instead of playing the
game. I'm sorry that I shoved Gwen. I said I was sorry then,
and I am really sorry about that.

**Jamie:** So it sounds like you both have valid points of view about
the situation.

## Step Three: Expressing Feelings

It's important to acknowledge that conflicts always involve
feelings. When there is enough trust to openly express feelings, the resolution process can move more quickly. Watch
for the tendency to fall into blaming at this stage. You want
each person to briefly share her feelings but not overexplain or
justify them.

**Jamie:** What feelings did this situation bring up for you?

**Anna:** I felt bad, kind of ashamed, I guess, that I shoved Gwen.
*(Anna stopped, blinking back tears.)* And, I don't know, I think
I felt frustrated or angry about changing the rules.

**Jamie:** Thanks, Anna. Gwen?

**Gwen:** I felt disrespected when Anna yelled and shoved me. And
sad. I guess angry, too.

**Jamie:** You both have some pretty strong feelings about the situation. Do you understand now where Anna is coming from,
Gwen? And Anna, do you have a better idea of how Gwen is
feeling? *(Both girls nod in agreement.)*

### Step Four: Sharing Responsibility

This step, often overlooked, is in my mind the most important in the process. Too often, conflict hits an impasse because the parties try to assign blame outside themselves. The conflict escalates when listening stops and each person justifies her "rightness." The truth is, in a conflict between two people, each person fuels the conflict. Perhaps one person bears 70 percent responsibility and the other 30 percent, but you're heading down a dead-end street if you're wrapped up in who is more right (and the flip side, who is more wrong). The critical move that breaks the impasse is a shift in focus from the other's behavior to one's own behavior. The *only* way to get past gridlock is for each person to "own" a piece of responsibility, reflect on her behavior, and resolve to act differently the next time. Most conflicts remain stuck because the focus is purely on what the other person did wrong. This leads to no learning and no change. During this step, it's time for the participants to look in the mirror. With Gwen and Anna, I asked a transformative question that shifted the conversation from finger pointing to a more accountable position.

> **Jamie:** What part did each of you play in the situation? In other words, how did you contribute to the situation?

After a minute or so, Anna spoke.

> **Anna:** I let my frustration get to me. I should have just said, "Whatever" and let go of how I wanted to play the game. It wasn't worth getting, like, really mad. And I made things much worse when I tried too hard to get the ball from Gwen by shoving her away.
>
> **Gwen:** Um, I guess I get really sensitive when Anna uses a tough voice with me. (*a few tears*) I start thinking that she doesn't like me anymore. Then I get kind of weird. I get sad and a little mad, and maybe that's why I really wanted to make

that shot. I get worried that Anna doesn't want to be friends. (*wipes away a tear*)

**Jamie:** Great—so now you recognize the role each of you played in this conflict.

## Step Five: Committing to Action

The insight that comes from step four is invaluable as a stepping-stone to resolution, but stopping there can still lead right back into gridlock. Only when habits change will a sustainable resolution be found. So I asked the girls, "What are you willing to do differently next time?" There was a long silence.

**Anna:** I will be more flexible about the rules, and if I get frustrated, I will go find another game to play. I don't mean in a mad sort of way—it's just that there are a lot of other games that go on at recess, and I can just find one that I want to play more. It's nothing personal to Gwen. And I will not shove or push Gwen again, ever.

**Gwen:** I'll stop myself from taking little things that happen on the playground as like, "Oh no, Anna doesn't like me anymore."

**Jamie:** It sounds like you're really serious about committing to a different behavior next time you run into this kind of conflict. How about if you check in with each other in a few days to see how you're doing on changing your reactions?

Gwen and Anna nodded.

## Step Six: Appreciating Each Other

At this point, most of the hard work is done, and it's time to affirm the relationship. To end on an encouraging note, Gwen and Anna shared how much they appreciate their friendship.

□□□

Whew. You may be wondering, *How can I keep all this in mind when going through my own conflicts with my kids or my spouse?* Here is a summary of the main things to remember during any conflict:

- Focus on areas of agreement to avoid polarizing around disagreement.
- Listen instead of only hearing things that justify your position.
- Try to see the conflict from the other person's perspective instead of getting stuck in blame.
- Acknowledge feelings, or else the conflict is unlikely to move to resolution.
- Look at what you bring to the conflict instead of just focusing on what the other person did wrong.
- Think about what you will do differently to avoid the conflict from recurring.
- Affirm the relationship by expressing your appreciation.

## CONFLICTS WITH PARTNERS

Whether you are living in the same house or separately, if two parents are involved in raising your child, you can't avoid coleadership challenges. Parents have different views and experiences related to raising a child. These differences are inevitable and beneficial but create a conundrum: How do you develop a healthy, separate identity distinct from your partner's and, at the same time, collaborate on and institute a joint vision and instill a unified set of values? The most influential lessons the child receives about interpersonal relationships come from how the parents work through their conflicts, so it's worth the effort to hone your coleadership skills.

Effective coleadership relies on four critical activities: gaining self-awareness about the influence of personal histories, fighting constructively, devoting time to the relationship, and learning to handle typical co-parenting challenges, such as distribution of household chores and differing disciplinary styles.

### Gaining Self-Awareness

Parents must recognize how their relationships with their own parents and with previous intimate partners carry over into their current union. The goal of every successful leader is to gain

---

## QUESTIONS FOR CO-PARENTS TO CONSIDER

- What were the male and female roles in your family of origin?

- In your family of origin, how were mothers working outside the home perceived? Did your mother work outside the home? What was her attitude about work? How does this influence your expectations of each other?

- What were each of your parents' modes—that is, Achiever, Connector, or Liberator? What are each of your modes? How does your mode play out in conflicts?

- How did your parents confront conflict with each other and with you?

- How was the labor of the household distributed?

After answering these questions, talk with your co-parent about how each of your families of origin might be playing a role in your conflicts. What factors in your upbringing do you want to embrace or discard in order to bring more health and harmony into your current family relationships?

control over past influences so that she is in the driver's seat, not driven by unconscious forces that haven't been properly worked out. There is nothing like becoming a parent to revive emotions from your family of origin. An important step in communicating effectively and becoming a healthy role model for your child is to gain awareness about unresolved feelings from your childhood in order to understand how your history influences your communication style, including your response to conflict. As you become more aware of the emotions that are triggered during conflict, you can bypass the traps that cause conflicts to fester and escalate. Successful parents and leaders make conscious choices to discard the family myths and internalized "scripts" that impede their interpersonal effectiveness.

It's valuable to reflect on how your upbringing influences how you handle parenting challenges. For example, David Green, father of Emma, six, recognized that when his mother was suffering from a terminal illness when he was a teenager, he received a message from his parents to "soldier on" and not give in to his fears. He realized that when his daughter expressed her fears of sleeping alone in her bed, his first reaction was impatience—why couldn't she just soldier on through the night? He needed to balance his internalized message with compassion for his daughter. This required working with his ex-wife, who was more apt to overconsole Emma when she was afraid. Together they planned their strategies—playing soothing music at night, rewarding their daughter when she slept in her own bed—in order to be leaders who facilitate Emma's development and work toward a joint vision: to foster self-reliance.

## Fighting Constructively

As is true of all parenting behavior, we set an example when we argue with our partners. Fighting is inevitable, but *how* we fight can make the difference in our child's emotional intelligence.

Arguing is guaranteed to be more constructive if you keep a few important things in mind:

- Don't dive in when you're in a highly emotional state of mind.
- Take time to calm down before engaging in conflict; during your time-out, find ways to see the situation from your partner's perspective in order to gain empathy.
- Instead of justifying your position of "rightness," find ways that your partner's position makes sense; identify the ways that you contributed to the conflict.
- Think big-picture: What is the goal of successful resolution? And don't say it's winning the argument! Instead, how about regaining compassion, strengthening connection, setting an example for your child, and finding common ground in order to move closer to a big-picture goal? Remember that positively resolving arguments benefits your child. The objective is not to avoid conflict (which is impossible anyway); rather, the key is to confront conflict respectfully and resolve arguments positively.

My husband and I are at our all-time worst during tax season. Around March, Burke becomes my tax man. His job is made harder by my self-employed status and poor bookkeeping skills. One day, he lost his patience with my mysterious invoicing system. We revved up into an emotionally charged fight. He bombarded me with anger-tinged questions I couldn't answer. I yelled, "I can't take this. I'm hiring my own accountant. Every year we go through this, and I'm sick and tired of it."

Our older daughter was in earshot of my high-volume, scornful tone. Bolstered by the recognition that Anna was witness to our conflict, I wanted a positive and also authentic resolution—not just to give Burke a false apology. My about-face was fueled by true respect for Burke, which I latched on to before escalating the conflict further. I also recognized that I felt guilty that he had spent this sunny Saturday on our taxes and that my disorganized bookkeeping practices made the process harder.

Through the fog of my own shame (I know my accounting practices are abysmal) and a strong distaste for all things quantitative, my reaction had been disrespectful anger. Shifting from my more impulsive response, I thanked Burke for spending his precious weekend hours figuring out our taxes. I told him I appreciated how much effort our taxes demand. And I hoped that the relatively quick turnaround—thanking Burke and validating his efforts—was teaching a valuable lesson to Anna and lifting Burke and me out of a recurring conflict.

---

## CO-PARENTING *NOT*-TO-DO LIST

Check any that sound familiar.

- ☐   You delegated lunches to your husband, but find yourself repacking them, mumbling under your breath, "It's Kira who likes apples and Chloe who like oranges. Sheesh, can't he do anything right?"

- ☐   You overturn your husband's ban on computer games when your child whines that she's so tired from her long day at school.

- ☐   You overhear your husband reading to your kids when it's past their bedtime. You waltz into their room and turn off the light, snapping, "Bedtime!"

- ☐   Your husband charges into the den where you're watching a TV show with your daughter. He says, "Sierra, your room's a mess, and I asked you to clean it up hours ago." You give your child a look to show you're allied with her, with Dad as the menacing outsider.

- ☐   Your daughter asks if she can get a kitten. You say *you'd* love to get a kitten, but remind her that Daddy thinks she's not old enough yet.

## Devoting Time to Your Relationship

When you're running around crazed and busy, your husband can easily get relegated to the sidelines. We've all heard it, but here it is again: the time you spend on your relationship helps your children. If we're big-picture parents, we recognize that devoting every waking hour to our children or our work and letting our relationship atrophy leaves our children at risk. There's nothing like a thriving marriage to teach your child about love, respect, and cooperation. Such a relationship can't exist without your setting time aside to nourish it. Putting the marriage on hold until the kids are grown isn't exactly a workable strategy. Even if you aren't married, the civility of your relationship with your ex is still key to your child's well-being. Here are some tips to fortify your relationship:

- Think gratitude. What do you love about your spouse? Tell him.
- What's on your spouse's mind? If you don't know, ask.
- Schedule time for pleasurable activities—just the two of you. Rediscover things you enjoyed before you had children.
- Spend time *every day* to talk about the day and express appreciation. Even if you're divorced, isn't there something you appreciate about how your ex is helping to raise your child? Express thanks, even if simply for the sake of your child. Especially if you are separated or divorced, it's important to check in each day about what happened in your child's life.

## Handling Typical Challenges Well

The most common complaint I hear from working mothers is that they still pull a second shift when they get home from work and that their parenting duties don't stop when they go to work. Even with parents who make a concerted effort to divide the job equally, and even though research shows that fathers spend far more time on housework than they did a decade ago, the lion's share still seems to fall on Mom. So how can we women deal with the stress-inducing chores that are still disproportionately ours?

Here's what I've learned from leading parenting groups. If you want your partner to share more in the work, respect and mutual regard are essential. As I mentioned earlier in the book, women often say that their male partners are better able to compartmentalize, meaning that when they go to work, they're at work, whereas moms are at work but also multitasking—scheduling doctor's appointments, e-mailing to arrange play dates, and searching the Internet for summer camps. That men and women juggle work and home priorities differently doesn't mean men care less about parenting. Men appreciate it when their role as parent is respected as being different, but just as important.

*How you react to the different ways each of you comes to your role as parent is key:* Do you resent your husband's ability to compartmentalize? Do you resent your role as the family scheduler? I admit, I do—or I did. I had to change my ways (still a work in progress) when I noticed that my resentment about doing more of the household work led me to criticize my husband whenever he did try to take on domestic tasks. I need to let go of my control, take time to divide up tasks, and accept that I *choose* to assume certain responsibilities, such as volunteering on the field trips, arranging the play dates, and going to the doctor appointments. In fact, I often discourage my husband from doing these tasks because I want to do them myself. It helps to step back and see how you might be discouraging your husband's involvement in the domestic chores by being critical or controlling when he does step in.

## Having Different Disciplinary Styles

Another big source of marital discord is that one parent is more lenient, the other more strict. This can play out in ways that polarize parents. For example, Michael, an executive at a bank and a very involved father, married to Barbara, also a busy executive, describes the different ways they deal with their dual responsibilities.

"I think Barbara is more lenient than I am because she feels guilty being away from our child so much. That means I'm often the one who has to play the bad cop when our daughter misbehaves." Both Barbara and Michael are committed parents, and their child knows she is well loved, but their leadership styles are different. Ideally, two parents discipline consistently and take their bigger disagreements behind closed doors instead of undermining the authority of the other parent in front of the child. Child development research has shown that children without consistency are anxiety-ridden, aggressive, or depressed. If differences are dealt with respectfully, children can learn conflict resolution, compassion, and compromise.

In our family, I'm more lenient. If Leah is enjoying a TV show, I'm bound to cave in and let her continue to watch even after her requisite TV time is up. Burke, by contrast, has no problem hitting the power button midshow.

We all have clashes with our parenting partners. It's how we respond that matters. Do we pull our rank as Mom-in-Chief? Do we bite our tongue and then finally explode with anger? Here are some tips for managing your differences with mutual respect and dignity:

- Jointly decide on your collective "nonnegotiables" and stick to them. (For example, you might decide that you are going to allow no more than forty-five minutes a day of TV.)
- Refrain from undermining the other's authority.
- When you disagree, talk it over privately.
- If you negotiate in front of the kids, do so respectfully.
- Avoid pitting one parent against the other, falling into a good cop–bad cop routine.
- Agree to support the parent who begins a discipline by allowing him or her to follow through without your questioning or overturning the decision.

In the chapter ahead, we'll explore what all great leaders do: create healthy, vibrant cultures that promote harmony and foster shared responsibility. You'll learn to diagnose the culture of your family and see how it affects the day-to-day dynamics of your home life. You'll learn practices to build a culture of accountability, encourage cooperation, and foster success without imposing your agenda and causing needless stress—all powerful ways to build cohesive, respectful, happy families.

# LEADERSHIP STRATEGY 4

# Creating a Family Culture

I believe that cultures begin with leaders who impose their own values and assumptions on a group. . . . Cultural understanding is desirable for all of us, but it is essential to leaders if they are to lead.
—Edgar H. Schein, author of *Organizational Culture and Leadership*

Every family, like every company, has its own culture and collective personality. Culture, the norms and beliefs of a family or organization—*its way of being*—determines, in large part, how people make decisions, regard authority, assume responsibility, and handle conflict. Our goals and values are transmitted through our family's culture in a million unconscious ways, and they guide how our children deal with challenges, form relationships, and rear their own children.

When your family tells stories about Aunt Jenny, who immigrated to this country without a cent, went to college, and became a successful businesswoman, you're teaching your child the value of hard work and education. Maybe your family's dinner table debates are about global warming, the greatest Beatles album, or why more women aren't CEOs. These concerns will carry over to your children's own adult dinner tables. Perhaps burping at the table is tolerated, but saying "Shut up" elicits a sharp "We don't talk that way in this family." What you do and don't tolerate conveys to your child your views about courtesy and values. Every action, whether purposeful or not, can send a message with a lasting influence on your child's life.

## TAKING A CULTURAL TOUR

When I work with businesses, I take managers on "cultural tours" of their company. We walk through the lobby and notice how the surly security guard greets visitors. We make surprise visits to the company's retail stores to step into the experience of their customers. I encourage leaders to look at their work climate through the eyes of a curious anthropologist—to simply observe, without judgments: Who speaks most in meetings, what kind of people get hired, what gets rewarded and punished, how is information exchanged across departments, and how does the company celebrate success?

Similarly, when you take a cultural tour of your house, try to remain neutral and resist judgments. Simply listen, look around with a visitor's eye, and reflect. How do people respond to difficulty in your family? What messages are conveyed about learning and achievement? What happens when people make mistakes? What behavior is likely to elicit the most praise and delight? What behavior is scorned?

Just as when you visit a foreign country and realize how American you really are, when you visit another family, your culture's distinctiveness emerges.

I can remember the unique personalities of my friends' homes when I was a kid. I spent much of my time at Marina's house, which couldn't have been more different from my quiet house, occupied by just me, my mom, and our cat, Schroeder. Marina's house, by contrast, was action packed. Marina's father was often hovering over a huge bubbling pot of marinara sauce, singing arias at the top of his lungs in Italian, or yelling at us to go outside. The fighting between the siblings was constant and, to me as an only child, fascinating: "John did it." "No, it was Kevin." "You lie. Marina broke the window and she knows it!" "I did not!"

I envied them for all their chaos, a feeling that Marina, to this day, thinks is hilarious.

I learned a lot about my grown-up family's culture the summer when our friends and their two daughters from France stayed with us for a week. The first culture shock came when my girls jumped up and down on our couch in the den, inviting their French friends to join in the fun. Annae and Philae looked horrified.

"C'mon, it's fun!" yelled my older daughter.

They stared, wide-eyed and frozen. Finally, ten-year-old Annae politely announced, "We do not jump on couches in our family." Their family arrived at the dinner table each evening dressed in fine clothes. Our family's informality came into full view in a way it never had before, complete with deafening slurps and tomato sauce–slathered lips. I remember thinking to myself, *Do we always sound this loud at the dinner table?* When Leah's giggle fit reached a milk-spraying-out-of-the-mouth climax, I vowed to step up my dinner table decorum lessons. It's easier to notice your family's culture when you examine it through the eyes of a visitor. Sometimes you see a contrast that makes you appreciate your own culture. Other times you may see an opportunity for improvement.

## HEALTHY CULTURE

At work and in families, a healthy culture will promote a sense of belonging, mutual respect, and initiative. In contrast, an ailing culture can keep people from reaching their full potential. A strong, healthy culture is a lot like leadership itself: hard to put your finger on, but you know it when you see it.

There are three signs of a healthy culture I look for in companies: engagement, healthy conflict, and tolerance of mistakes.

### Engagement

A sense of belonging, emotional connection to the company's goals, and a feeling that you're valued are all hallmarks of a strong culture. I had my first experience in a company with a thriving culture when I worked at Levi Strauss. Even though I was fresh out of graduate school, people treated me with so much respect that I started to feel valuable and engaged. My boss assigned me to projects in which I could make a significant impact, and I eagerly assumed more responsibility. Even though I was unseasoned and making plenty of mistakes, I realized that my ideas mattered and that I could make a difference. Engagement cultures foster loyalty and motivation.

## Healthy Conflict

In strong cultures, people feel free to speak their minds without fear of retribution. Disagreement isn't relegated to hushed conversations at the watercooler. Great leaders realize that for a company to thrive, they must encourage healthy dissent. Instead of thwarting conflict, they cultivate lively debate, making it clear that people are not only able to express their views but also expected to question the boss and think critically. Let's look at what happens when conflict is suppressed.

A manager I coached, Evelyn, was frustrated by her staff's passivity during meetings. When I observed Evelyn in action, it became clear why people didn't speak up. The few times people did express an opinion, Evelyn shot it down with "That won't work" and other crushing responses. One employee summed up the group's perception of Evelyn: "She processes everything we say through a filter of judgment. She doesn't care what we think. She believes we're passive and have nothing valuable to add, but it's because she doesn't give us any true responsibility, so we have no choice but to be disengaged."

Your challenge as a parent is to find ways to reward your child for respectfully standing up for his own convictions and to remove restraints that stifle freedom of expression. It takes a conscious commitment to create a culture in which family members know that no matter how difficult conflict is, bringing it to the surface is more valuable that avoiding it.

## Tolerance of Mistakes

As we explored in Chapter One, the best leaders realize that with failures come the biggest growth opportunities. Companies with strong cultures find ways to encourage and even reward mistakes. DuPont's Textile Fibers Division awards a quarterly "failure trophy." DuPont realizes that achievements come as much, if not more, from failure as they do from success. Tom Watson Sr., the founder of IBM, was often quoted as saying, "The way to accelerate your rate of success is to double your failure rate."

One of the hardest things for many parents is to watch their child struggle or fail. In a child's world, failure can be as simple as spilling juice all over the table, losing a jacket, or getting stuck on a thorny math problem. As a leader, you need to watch how you react to mistakes. How you respond—your tone, your words—can send a message that either becomes an impediment to your child's confidence or creates a learning environment where your child feels free to experiment, take risks, and grow.

---

### CULTURAL ASSESSMENT

You can look for signs of healthy culture in your home, too. Read over the questions and, using a 1–5 scale (1 = to a very low extent; 5 = to a very high extent), circle the number that you feel best characterizes your family.

1. Engagement
   - To what extent do people feel respected and appreciated and that their opinion matters?

   1          2          3          4          5

   - To what extent is there a sense of cohesion and esprit de corps?

   1          2          3          4          5

- To what extent do people take initiative and cooperate to support the family's common goals and values?

  1   2   3   4   5

- To what extent do celebrations feel meaningful and cultivate a sense of community?

  1   2   3   4   5

2. Healthy conflict
   - To what extent do people feel free to disagree?

     1   2   3   4   5

   - To what extent is open, direct communication the norm?

     1   2   3   4   5

   - To what extent do people share their feelings honestly?

     1   2   3   4   5

   - To what extent are conflicts brought to the surface in a timely manner and resolved?

     1   2   3   4   5

3. Tolerance of mistakes
   - To what extent do people view failure as a path to success?

     1   2   3   4   5

- To what extent is misbehavior viewed as an opportunity for growth?

  1          2          3          4          5

- To what extent do people feel free to share their mistakes and learn from them?

  1          2          3          4          5

- To what extent are mistakes confronted in a nonjudgmental manner and followed up with clear expectations?

  1          2          3          4          5

☐ ☐ ☐

Add up the numbers of each response to get your grand total:_____. If your total score is 48 or higher, congratulations. Your culture consists of many of the ingredients required for a healthy culture. A response of 1 or 2 indicates an area that could use some strengthening. If your total score is 24 or below, it's time to talk with your family about ways to revitalize your culture. Pick one area in each section with relatively low numbers and write down what you plan to do to make improvements. Strengthening one area will often trigger a chain reaction, creating significant positive change in your overall culture.

## BOLD ACTIONS STRENGTHEN CULTURE

Once you gain an understanding of your culture, you'll need to take bold and purposeful action to make improvements and reinforce your values. This is the hallmark of leadership.

Lecturing won't get the job done. What's important in building a day-to-day healthy culture is setting a strong example by walking your talk. The most effective leaders often go beyond business as usual to send a culture-strengthening message.

Jan Carlzon, CEO of Scandinavian Airlines System (SAS), made a spectacular display of how much he values creativity and customer service when he noticed that managers in his company were overrelying on rule books instead of making thoughtful decisions with the customer's best interest in mind. Instead of convening a meeting to give a pep talk about his values, Carlzon burned thousands of pages of rule books. To demonstrate his deeply held value of equality, he got rid of the company's executive dining room. These dramatic acts not only made the impact he desired but also became part of the company's folklore, passed down to new employees to teach them about SAS's principles.

Putting action behind your words is just as important in your home. You say you want your kid to value social justice, but when was the last time you served lunch at the local soup kitchen? You want your kids to care about their environment, but you can't be bothered to install low-energy light bulbs in your home. You want your son to be self-sufficient, but you still pack his lunch every day.

Barbara King, a manager and the mom of two sons, didn't like the values she saw conveyed on her children's favorite TV shows. So she pulled the plug on TV. "I got fed up with commercials selling products to my children, and insipid characters who value looks over brains, so first I told the kids there would be no TV for a week." For the first two days, they missed TV, but by the end of the week they found things to do that they enjoyed more than sitting in front of a TV screen. Barbara's husband had the hardest time giving up television. But they decided together that if they really wanted to walk the talk, they both had to stick to their priorities. They eventually got rid of the TV altogether.

Not all of us are cut out for pulling the plug on TV, but I'm sure you have your own strong values that you can reinforce with bold actions. The most effective leaders take courageous stands that go beyond platitudes and create a lasting impact.

## THE VALUE OF CELEBRATIONS

Celebrating is one powerful way you can convey your family's values and foster a healthy culture. You may have worked for an organization that makes a lot of hoopla when the company hits a milestone or someone does something that demonstrates a corporate value. Companies with healthy cultures understand the huge benefits that come from meaningful celebrations. Notice the word *meaningful*. Events that feel forced or inauthentic can backfire, causing cynicism. But when done right, celebrations and rituals convey sincere appreciation and reinforce the company's values. There's no great mystery behind the power of celebrations. All of us want to feel recognized by others. When we feel appreciated, we feel a greater sense of connection and commitment.

Celebrations need a personal touch to make a difference. Recall an occasion when you received a meaningless certificate for something at an impersonal ceremony. How did it feel? Now think about a time when your boss recognized *you*, or threw a celebratory event that felt special and sincere, not slapdash or obligatory. It felt good, didn't it?

Whenever Barclays Global Investors (BGI) launches a new product, for instance, it's time for a celebration to recognize everyone's hard work. Daniel Morillo, manager of an investment group within BGI, noticed that people were working long hours to launch a new fund, so he decided to recognize their hard work and give them a much-needed break. The first celebration, a dinner at a fine restaurant, was so well received that he decided to have regular celebrations: an afternoon of go-cart racing, a book exchange, and other original activities that were customized around his staff's unique interests. He made a point of tailoring creative celebrations so that they weren't obligatory, but personal and meaningful.

It's well understood that in high-performing organizations, ceremonies and celebrations convey values and invigorate corporate culture. The same is true for families. Celebrations make people feel good. You can take a moment to think about the kinds of celebrations you have in your home.

- Are there opportunities for celebrations that you might try that go beyond the expected birthdays and holidays?
- Do you involve your children in planning celebrations?
- Are there things you can do to make celebrations more engaging and meaningful?

It takes a conscious effort to demonstrate actions that create the family culture you want for your children. As a business leader or parent, you set the tone. You are the culture captain.

The first step in creating the culture you want is to understand the culture in which you live. Then you're able to reinforce the aspects you like and remedy the ailing parts of your culture. Give your organization and family a culture checkup—in other words, notice if there's anything you need to fix. See if any of the following descriptions of unhealthy cultures remind you of dynamics you experience in your workplace or your home.

## UNHEALTHY CULTURE

When assessing companies, I look for telltale signs of an unhealthy culture, such as disengaged employees and discord between management and staff. All families and organizations have their share of cultural maladies. The three most common types of unhealthy cultural patterns are

1. Disengaged: "It's not my fault"
2. Command-and-control: "Do it because I said so"
3. Competitive: "My child's going to Yale"

### Disengaged: "It's Not My Fault"

You may have worked in a company where excuses, blame, and confusion are the default reactions whenever problems arise. The ultimate problem when you have a disengaged culture is that more and more energy goes into evading responsibility, leaving less energy available to make changes and meet desired outcomes. People feel powerless and at the mercy of life's circumstances.

Disengaged cultures are filled with "victims" who make excuses when they mess up instead of taking responsibility for their actions. We all know victims: they're the ones who blame everyone and everything for their lot in life. They wallow in self-pity and make excuses rather than assuming ownership of the role they play in their life's circumstances. Disengagement weakens both businesses and families.

Over the years, I've worked with many people caught in a cycle of disengagement. The signs are the same: denial of personal responsibility, excuses, finger pointing, and confusion. One manager I coached, dispirited after getting fired for the second time in five years, epitomized disengagement. When I asked him why he had lost his jobs, he was ready with rationalizations crafted to convince everyone (including himself) that getting fired wasn't his fault. Here's a partial list of his excuses:

"The board was inept and wanted me to do the impossible."

"My boss kept changing his expectations of me. I was never given any clear goals"

"The employees have gotten away with being incompetent for years. No one will admit that it will take some sort of magic potion to turn things around."

"Both organizations had the same problem—disgruntled workers who whine and take no initiative and then, in I come, a perfect opportunity to redirect blame for their irresponsibility."

"I was just the scapegoat. They created the mess and then they point fingers at me."

I'm sure there was some legitimacy to his claims, but until this manager could take at least partial ownership for his part, he was in for more of the same in the future. To shift from a disengaged mentality takes courage to look at your own behavior, recognize how you contributed to the problem, and then change habits. Unfortunately, in the case of this particular manager, the more I encouraged him to take some responsibility for his predicament so that he could learn and grow, the more aggressive his rationalizations became, until he and I parted ways. I assumed he would make the same mistakes over and over again until perhaps the patterns became too glaringly obvious for him to remain in denial.

A disengaged culture can take root at home too. The symptoms?

Whining ("Why do I have to feed the cat?")

Excuses ("I left my bike outside because I was late.")

Blaming ("Serena made me do it.")

Denying responsibility ("It's Anna's turn to set the table.")

Here are more classic lines you are likely to hear in a disengaged culture (I confess, these are all examples from my own house):

"I *did* put my jacket in the closet. Someone must have taken it."

"Why do *I* always have to set the table?"

"I would have cleaned my room, but you told me I had to do my homework."

"It's not my fault."

"I couldn't help it."

The antidote to a disengaged culture is an infusion of accountability. There are three powerful strategies to teach your child to be more accountable: stop covering for your child; teach accountability; and praise effort, not talent.

### Stop Covering

At one of my talks, Angelina, a brave mom struggling with her Connector mode run amok (see Mom Modes in Leadership Strategy 2), shared that she really wanted to stop rescuing her daughter from the consequences of her own forgetfulness.

"The other day, she forgot her homework. This is after I reminded her, *just that morning*, to put her homework in her backpack. I threatened not to go and get it even when she told me the teacher would mark her grade down. But when I saw the crestfallen look on her face, I caved. I told her that was the last time I'd do that. Two days later, she forgot her homework again. Unbelievable! And guess what? I retrieved it again!" said Angelina.

Kids don't learn from threats; they learn from experience. One mom said her son, seventeen, made an agreement about how much money he could spend each week. He never adhered to the plan. "We reprimanded him . . . and kept giving him more money. He had constant excuses. Nothing worked until the money stopped."

I struggle to stand firm on chores. In our house, we're good about chores to a point. The girls design and decorate chore charts, hang them on the refrigerator, and dutifully mark off when they complete their tasks. But busy schedules take over (I know, that's an excuse), and before long, I'm setting the table and my husband is taking out the recycling, and all the while we're muttering to each other, "Isn't this their job?" My husband and I have to remind ourselves about the big-picture reason we delegate chores—to instill responsibility and build a sense of community spirit at home—or else we take the short view and do the chores ourselves instead of battling the excuses. I know better than to tolerate this kind of victim mindset at work. Would I delegate a project to an employee and then do it myself? I don't think so. I need to remember to take the same kinds of vision-embodying stands with our children in order to prevent disengagement from creeping into our home.

### Teach Accountability

Nora's six-year-old daughter, Thalia, prone to drama, came home from school each day with a tale of woe. Her friends were being mean to her. "My friends are all mean and I hate them. They don't play with me, so I have to sit all by myself on the bench during recess," said Thalia. Nora listened and tried comforting her daughter, to no avail. Fortunately, Nora had the wherewithal to notice that her child was taking no responsibility for the problems with her friends and began to wonder if there was more to her story.

After she helped Thalia express her desire—to play and have fun with her friends—Nora probed for a few more details: Thalia wanted her friends to play four-square, yet all they wanted to play was freeze tag, which, according to Thalia, was "the stupidest game in the world." Finally, Nora asked her daughter two questions that changed Thalia's attitude: (1) Is there anything you can do differently so that you're having more fun with your friends at recess? (2) What choices do you have in this situation? Thinking about these questions, Thalia realized that she had a choice in the situation and had the power to influence a different outcome. With her mom's guidance, Thalia came to see that her inflexibility was part of the problem. She was sitting on the bench alone because she chose to, not because her friends excluded her from their games. If she compromised and played what the other girls wanted to play, she would no longer sit alone at recess. Once she recognized how she was contributing to the problem, she was able to abandon her "poor me" attitude and take ownership of the role she played in her predicament. In other words, she was able to see that she had a *choice* in the matter, which meant that she could choose a different reaction and get a different result.

When you hear things like "It's not my fault," "I got a D because I suck at math," or "My friends treat me badly," to foster accountability you can ask, "What might you do differently next time?" or "What part did you play?" or "Is there something you can do to influence the situation?" All these questions prompt your child to focus attention on the aspects of the situation she can control—her attitude and behavior—thus enabling her to shape the consequences of her actions.

### Praise Effort, Not Talent

What sets successful people apart from others is drive. To foster an engagement culture, you need to help your child understand the connection between effort and success—that success comes only after lots of really hard work. Remember how Carol Dwerk,

---

## WATCH YOUR LANGUAGE

| Disengaged Language | Accountable Language |
| --- | --- |
| He's a born athlete. | He practices daily. |
| Eli's the social one, and Landon is the smart one. | Eli puts a lot of energy into his friendships. Landon puts more effort into his schoolwork. |
| I didn't win the race. That's not fair. | I didn't win the race, but I did my best. |
| I'll never get promoted because I'm not a people person. | I need to work on my interpersonal skills so that I can get promoted to a more challenging position. |
| I failed my math test. I'm horrible at math. | I failed my math test because I didn't study very hard. |

the Stanford psychologist we met in Leadership Strategy 1, found in her research that praising talent alone undermines success by conveying a fixed mindset message? It's tempting to praise your child's talents, but talent alone can be a curse. If your family culture has promoted the idea that success is based on inborn talent, your child will get disengaged the minute he confronts challenge, thinking that his failure reveals that he really isn't talented after all, so why try. Kids who believe that their success is based on innate talent are reluctant to take on challenging tasks for fear that their gift will be called into question if they don't excel. In contrast, if your child understands that effort is essential for success, he can persevere after he hits difficulties. Successful business leaders believe that their job is to help people confront challenges and grow to reach their potential. Successful parents believe the same thing.

One way to put this belief into action is to point out how effort, not merely talent, leads to success. When my daughter and I went to a Hilary Hahn violin concert, we talked afterward about how many hours each day she must practice to be able to play like that. Sure, she has inborn talent, but no one can play Vivaldi the way she does with talent alone. It's like that old joke attributed to the great violinist Isaac Stern, who responded to a tourist's question on the street—"How do I get to Carnegie Hall?"—with "Practice! Practice! Practice!"

Great leaders believe in human potential. They promote growth by insisting that people assume responsibility for their actions, keep commitments, and persevere when confronted with challenge.

## Command-and-Control: "Do It Because I Said So"

In a command-and-control culture, people perceive a lack of power and the means to effect change. Leaders in command-and-control cultures operate under the worn-out assumption that people in authority have the answers and that if you give people power, chaos ensues. Respect is given lip service while people's need for participation goes unmet. Adults like to feel trusted and empowered, and they resist being controlled. So do children.

One afternoon, I walked into a company headquarters to meet the director of a twelve-person information technology department. The director (I'll call him Jim) had sought my help with concerns about high employee turnover. Jim complained that his staff did only the bare minimum, clocked out at 4:59, and took no initiative. When I interviewed his team members individually, they all had the same story. They experienced Jim as intimidating, punishing, and critical. He was intolerant of mistakes or anyone disagreeing with him, he made decisions without any clear rationale aside from "because I said so," and he showed little curiosity about other people's ideas. Even ordering paper clips required his signature. Those who had recently left the company told me they had felt undervalued, harshly judged, and micromanaged.

After several months of coaching, Jim had an epiphany that changed the way he led at home and at work. At one of our morning meetings, Jim looked shell-shocked. He told me that after a fiery argument, his sixteen-year-old son, Mark, had moved out to live with his older sister. Jim realized that Mark sounded just like his employees, saying that he had had it with his father's criticism and punishments. Then Jim told me something else— that he had moved out of his parents' house at sixteen, fed up with his father's harsh and authoritarian ways. To my surprise, my client began to transform into a more compassionate leader. I don't want to minimize the hard work and pain Jim went through to change his leadership style. He remained tough, with exacting standards, but also with strengthened self-awareness; having experienced a wake-up call that forced him to recognize the impact of his behavior, he grew more flexible and empathic. Mark never moved back home, but their relationship improved markedly, as did the relationships between Jim and his staff.

When Jim discarded his command-and-control tactics, his department changed for the better faster than I would have imagined. He instituted flexible work schedules, which employees had asked for over the years. At meetings, he asked more questions and monitored how much he talked. Instead of saying no right away, which was his natural response, he asked people's opinions and guided them to their own solutions. When they came up with a solution different than the one he had in mind, he gave them the flexibility to do it their way as long as they achieved agreed-on results.

### Avoid Wielding Power

Children yearn for independence and involvement just as adults do in the workplace. When thwarted, they either fight or grow apathetic. As in the workplace, when parents wield power and fail to offer opportunities to be involved, children fail to engage, or they engage in disruptive ways. In a research study of youth conducted by the University of Minnesota, those who felt that they had the power to influence the conditions of their day-to-day lives were more positive and engaged than their peers who didn't feel respected. It's no surprise that children want the same thing from their institutions that adults want from theirs: meaningful roles, the experience of garnering appreciation, and the ability to use their voices to participate in creating their school and community environments.

Of course there are times when you have to pull the Mom-in-Chief card and make a unilateral decision "because I said so." But the mistake many parents make is to continue using the command-and-control approach that worked when their kid was two, even though the kid is now ten. The power-down approach does not work when a child is old enough to want a say in the matter. For her to comply feels to your child as if she were losing her sense of self. Remember, kids learn when they experience the consequences of their choices. What's the worst-case scenario if your child refuses to wear a jacket, despite your telling him it's freezing outside? Your child gets cold.

### Encourage Participation

If we cast away the old-school leadership mindset—in which leaders believe they need to tell people what to do or else they will behave badly—we're free to trust that people want to contribute and do their best. The most effective leaders realize that when you trust people and value their input, they rise to your expectations. Your job as a leader is to nourish people's capacity to solve their own problems and be involved in decisions. The leadership challenge for parents is to find appropriate opportunities for children to make choices.

### Encourage Involvement

In business, when people don't feel heard, they rebel, become apathetic, or find another job. The most effective leaders, no matter what the environment, nourish people's sense of involvement.

Rondi, a project manager at a research institute, is widely admired for her ability to encourage her colleagues' involvement. Her staff say that Rondi truly values what they have to say. Cathy B., an analyst, says, "I shared an idea with her once, and I'll never forget how she listened so intently. After hearing me out, she helped me get my idea published in a paper. It's almost unheard of for nonacademics to be published in this journal, but Rondi advocated for me."

Rondi's colleagues not only feel deeply appreciated for their ideas but also enlist in her vision of the institute. Rondi seeks input both to make people feel appreciated for their contribution and because she knows that if she imposed her own agenda without input, her decisions would be stripped of the diversity of ideas others have to offer. Furthermore, her staff wouldn't understand the ins and outs of the projects they work on, and they wouldn't feel a part of the plan's success.

Just like adults in a workplace, kids need to feel heard. You can engage children in the running of the household in all sorts of ways. Your child can design chore charts, propose ideas to help the environment, produce menus for the week, and come up with an itinerary for a fun-filled family day.

Sarah, a mom in my workshop, was out of patience with mealtime struggles. She accommodated her daughter's pickiness by making a select few bland dinners, but she knew there had to be a way to enjoy dinners more and get her daughter to eat a wider range of foods. Then she had an idea. She asked her daughter if she wanted to help her choose menus each week and cook meals together. Her daughter was initially wary until she proposed they go to the bookstore and buy a children's cookbook. Her daughter's idea worked like a charm. They found a cookbook and started to cook together. Surprising to both of them, their repertoire of palatable meals grew, and mealtime became less a battlefield and more a time for collaboration and fun.

### Conduct Family Meetings

The best tool I know for promoting involvement and esprit de corps is the family meeting. In my family, we hold meetings every week, and the kids are usually cheerful about attending. If one of our daughters has an issue on her mind, she is eager to remind us that it's Sunday and time to meet. Admittedly, there are times when I get the do-we-have-to-do-this expression, but once we begin, everyone gets engaged. On those Sunday evenings when I sense resistance, I start with an easier topic, such as where we want to go for our summer vacation, or whether to have a movie night—popcorn, daughter picks the movie, invites friends. I make sure our meetings are informal and fun, but we don't veer away from difficult issues. Everyone needs to know that when issues arise, they can be aired each week and will get the attention they deserve.

I haven't come across a better method for soliciting input, teaching conflict resolution, practicing gratitude, and creating a sense of being on the same team. Our first meetings, when my daughters were six and ten, were filled with silliness, giggling, and silence. Now our children have learned how to express themselves more clearly, convey their appreciation or frustration, advocate for themselves, negotiate, and clarify their point of view when they are challenged.

Here's how a family meeting works:

1. *Set simple ground rules:* don't interrupt, listen with respect, value all ideas, and try to understand what people are saying before jumping in with your point of view.

2. *Share appreciations.* In numerous surveys and studies, employees rank feeling appreciated much higher than salary in terms of what is most important for their satisfaction at work. Families are no different. In sociologist Christine Carter's family, she makes a daily practice of asking her kids to share what they're thankful for. A benefit, she says, is that they learn to constantly scan their environment to notice what they appreciate, enhancing their happiness. "People who practice gratitude have more energy, are happier, and are perceived as kinder," says Christine.

I brought two fun practices into our family that I've seen have tremendous benefit in the workplace. When I worked at the Tom Peters Group, we had sticky notes that said, "You Made My Day." I found myself constantly noticing people doing things I was thankful for. As hokey as it sounds, people loved receiving and giving these notes. We pass around You Made My Day thank-you notes in our family as well.

Another family favorite: we post four flipchart sheets on the wall, each sheet with one family member's name. Throughout the week, we write things on each person's sheet that we appreciate about him or her. At the end of the week, we read them together. This practice has truly made a difference in spreading a happy feeling in our house throughout the week.

3. *Share issues.* Anna doesn't like that Leah refuses to pick her clothes up off their bedroom floor, and Leah wants to trade her recycling chore for table setting. With a little coaching, our daughters are better able to share problems without blaming and come up with helpful solutions themselves.

4 *Share ideas for family activities.* For example, we've come up with family Scrabble night, weekly ice cream sundaes, more family bike rides, and a list of five new ways to cut down on waste and pollution in our home.

5. *Set up the weekly calendar.* This is how we always end our meeting. A popular innovation was the purchase of a whiteboard and markers to write reminders and schedules for the week.

### Establish Specific Expectations

In organizations, I find that the most collaborative and productive work groups establish clear expectations for how they want to operate as a team. They are diligent about measuring not just *what* they want to accomplish, but *how* they want to go about their work. For example, a team that complained that their meetings were disintegrating into low-energy wastes of time created a specific expectation; they wanted their group to be more interactive and collaborative. They initiated one simple change: they replaced all information-only agenda items with daunting obstacles that they needed to solve together in order to achieve their goals. People started to share challenges they faced in their work. Their meetings shifted from time wasters to lively problem-solving discussions.

You can establish measurable expectations and strategies to achieve them with your family too. Mary Anna, mother of two sons and three daughters, was tired of her kids' constant bickering and whining. She devised a method to begin to sense of the big picture. When a mom's sense of worth depends on her child's getting the starring role in the school play or scoring goals on an elite soccer team, it's time to step back and ask, *What do I really care about? What are my long-term goals?* When the anxiety gets so overwhelming that a mom loses sleep when her kid gets passed over for the advanced orchestra, there's something out of whack, and it's hurting both kids and parents.

## Changing Competitive Culture

John Yokoyama, owner of the World Famous Pike Place Fish Market in Seattle, understands the harm that can come from creating a competitive culture. When he opened his business, his sole purpose was to sell fish and pull in a sizable profit. When he first started his market, he viewed his staff as faceless objects whose only function was to achieve his agenda for success, which was profit, period. Employee theft, high staff turnover, and rampant drug use threatened to put him out of business. He made several mistakes common to a competitive culture: he failed to find ways to infuse meaning into his employees' daily toil; he imposed his agenda, treating his employees as commodities; he failed to get to know his staff as people; and he refused to provide them with meaningful input into the daily workings of his market. He was so busy striving for his version of success that he lost all sense of joy and fun—and so did his staff.

How did he turn his business into the most profitable fish business in the country? He saw that employee morale was in the toilet and that there was increasing criminality in the workplace. So he did a very smart thing. He changed the culture. He altered his purpose: instead of striving only to increase profits, he sought to make a difference in the lives of his employees and customers. By changing his definition of success and tapping into the interests, ideas, and passions of his employees, he enlisted his staff in his vision to create a world-famous fish market based on employee individuality, humor, joy, and an athletic sense of reckless abandon that truly reflects the culture of his

change the frustrating aspects of her family's culture. She had her family brainstorm the elements of ideal family expectations, and together they came up with a list that included respect, social responsibility, cooperation, and kindness. Then they took one item each month and defined it with specific behaviors. For example, November featured respect (we wash the dishes after eating; we listen without interrupting when someone is speaking; we all pitch in to clean the house; when we see a mess, we clean it up together, no matter who made it). For December the theme was social responsibility (we recycle to help the earth; we choose a community service activity; we contribute a portion of our allowance to a charity that we all decide on together).

"Our family felt more cohesive after this exercise. We have more fun together," said Mary Anna.

## Competitive: "My Kid's Going to Yale"

In many families, raising kids has become a competitive sport. If the popularity of bumper stickers that boast children's academic achievements is any indication, we live in a culture where honor roll status, test scores, and grades are prized above the joy of learning. Thousands of parents have resorted to software programs that allow them to track their child's daily school progress, including grades, attendance, class conduct, and missed assignments. Parental involvement has long been shown as an important aspect of academic success, but when taken to the extreme, the benefits evaporate. When parents use these software programs obsessively, they're conveying to their kids messages that run counter to transformational leadership: I don't trust you; you need my vigilant involvement or you won't stay on track; I'm not confident in your ability to succeed on your own; and as Denise Pope, Stanford professor of education said in an interview with the *New York Times*, "It's more important to get the grade, by hook or by crook, than learn the material." She goes on to say that these practices exert pressure that leads to rampant cheating.

I'm not saying every parent who uses this technology harms her child. If used appropriately, it can enhance teacher-parent communication. When used to excess and for the wrong reasons, however, this kind of micromanaging deprives a child of the learning required to be a self-reliant adult.

It's nice when our kids succeed, but if a parent's sense of self-worth is tied up too tightly with her kid's accomplishments, there will be problems. Parents who treat children as extensions of themselves have become such a widespread phenomenon that there is a recommendation in the psychiatric community to create a diagnosis called Achievement by Proxy Syndrome. If you're finding any of this uncomfortably familiar, it may be time to scale back your Achiever mode.

### Problems of Competitive Culture

There are three major problems with the competition culture. First, when parents emphasize results—for example, the straight A report card—children and parents lose sight of the most important thing: the joy of learning for learning's sake. Similarly, when winning a game takes center stage, the joyful simplicity of having fun or performing well gets subverted.

Second, in a competitive culture, children can feel that their parent's love is conditional, dependent on what they *do*—meet their parent's expectations. Children begin to see their sense of worth connected to whether they get the A, score the goal, or make the team. Most parents in my classes say they want to raise happy children, but these same parents sometimes send a message that they want their child to be successful on their terms. One mother told me with pride that her ten-year-old daughter was going to go to her alma mater, Yale. I asked, "What if she doesn't want to go to Yale?" Her response was, "Are you kidding? She's going to Yale!" I doubt that she set out to diminish her child's happiness, but I had to wonder how things will play out if her daughter decides she'll be happier at art school or, like the majority of applicants, doesn't get into Yale.

A young student I know named Delia, fourteen, expl[...] her motivation to study hard for her advanced placement [...] exams: "I don't want to let my parents down." Children wi[...] develop a strong sense of self-worth when their value goes u[...] down depending on how well they perform on a test or at a g[...]

The third problem with the competitive culture is [...] we're burdening children with crazy amounts of pressure. [...] Jackson, seventeen, watches his friends flip out at night. "L[...] my friends come home from school saying they need a dri[...] calm down. They feel like they have to take all AP classe[...] they have to get perfect test scores. My friends are so str[...] out," says Kyle.

In the midst of all this kid stress, parents lose out as [...] Regan McMahon, mom of Kyle and Hayley, fourteen, [...] author of *Revolution in the Bleachers*, a book that document[...] excesses in the competitive youth sports culture, says, "The [...] ents I interviewed for the book are living through their [...] Parents will say, '*We* have a lot of homework, or *we* los[...] game.'" When a kid does well in the game, McMahon says[...] the parent who feels a surge in self-worth. But if the kid's [...] loses, the parents are crushed, defeated, and depressed. The[...] the ones who feel like failures. Says McMahon, "We have t[...] a mirror up to the culture and ask is this the best we can [...] our kids and ourselves."

I interviewed kids who say they worry what their parents[...] think if they get a B instead of straight A's. Sarah, sevent[...] regularly turns down weekend recreational activities in [...] to study, write papers, and practice ballet (which has bec[...] a chore, but which she continues for the sake of her co[...] application and her parent's approval). Sarah tells me, "I g[...] I do feel like things are better with my parents when I get g[...] grades. And my dad definitely wants me to go to a better sc[...] than he went to."

Moms who are busy pushing their kids with agendas for [...] cess or falling prey to crazy societal expectations can lose[...]

change the frustrating aspects of her family's culture. She had her family brainstorm the elements of ideal family expectations, and together they came up with a list that included respect, social responsibility, cooperation, and kindness. Then they took one item each month and defined it with specific behaviors. For example, November featured respect (we wash the dishes after eating; we listen without interrupting when someone is speaking; we all pitch in to clean the house; when we see a mess, we clean it up together, no matter who made it). For December the theme was social responsibility (we recycle to help the earth; we choose a community service activity; we contribute a portion of our allowance to a charity that we all decide on together).

"Our family felt more cohesive after this exercise. We have more fun together," said Mary Anna.

## Competitive: "My Kid's Going to Yale"

In many families, raising kids has become a competitive sport. If the popularity of bumper stickers that boast children's academic achievements is any indication, we live in a culture where honor roll status, test scores, and grades are prized above the joy of learning. Thousands of parents have resorted to software programs that allow them to track their child's daily school progress, including grades, attendance, class conduct, and missed assignments. Parental involvement has long been shown as an important aspect of academic success, but when taken to the extreme, the benefits evaporate. When parents use these software programs obsessively, they're conveying to their kids messages that run counter to transformational leadership: I don't trust you; you need my vigilant involvement or you won't stay on track; I'm not confident in your ability to succeed on your own; and as Denise Pope, Stanford professor of education said in an interview with the New York Times, "It's more important to get the grade, by hook or by crook, than learn the material." She goes on to say that these practices exert pressure that leads to rampant cheating.

I'm not saying every parent who uses this technology harms her child. If used appropriately, it can enhance teacher-parent communication. When used to excess and for the wrong reasons, however, this kind of micromanaging deprives a child of the learning required to be a self-reliant adult.

It's nice when our kids succeed, but if a parent's sense of self-worth is tied up too tightly with her kid's accomplishments, there will be problems. Parents who treat children as extensions of themselves have become such a widespread phenomenon that there is a recommendation in the psychiatric community to create a diagnosis called Achievement by Proxy Syndrome. If you're finding any of this uncomfortably familiar, it may be time to scale back your Achiever mode.

### Problems of Competitive Culture

There are three major problems with the competition culture. First, when parents emphasize results—for example, the straight A report card—children and parents lose sight of the most important thing: the joy of learning for learning's sake. Similarly, when winning a game takes center stage, the joyful simplicity of having fun or performing well gets subverted.

Second, in a competitive culture, children can feel that their parent's love is conditional, dependent on what they *do*—meet their parent's expectations. Children begin to see their sense of worth connected to whether they get the A, score the goal, or make the team. Most parents in my classes say they want to raise happy children, but these same parents sometimes send a message that they want their child to be successful on their terms. One mother told me with pride that her ten-year-old daughter was going to go to her alma mater, Yale. I asked, "What if she doesn't want to go to Yale?" Her response was, "Are you kidding? She's going to Yale!" I doubt that she set out to diminish her child's happiness, but I had to wonder how things will play out if her daughter decides she'll be happier at art school or, like the majority of applicants, doesn't get into Yale.

A young student I know named Delia, fourteen, explained her motivation to study hard for her advanced placement (AP) exams: "I don't want to let my parents down." Children will not develop a strong sense of self-worth when their value goes up and down depending on how well they perform on a test or at a game.

The third problem with the competitive culture is that we're burdening children with crazy amounts of pressure. Kyle Jackson, seventeen, watches his friends flip out at night. "Lots of my friends come home from school saying they need a drink to calm down. They feel like they have to take all AP classes and they have to get perfect test scores. My friends are so stressed out," says Kyle.

In the midst of all this kid stress, parents lose out as well. Regan McMahon, mom of Kyle and Hayley, fourteen, and author of *Revolution in the Bleachers*, a book that documents the excesses in the competitive youth sports culture, says, "The parents I interviewed for the book are living through their kids. Parents will say, 'We have a lot of homework, or we lost the game.'" When a kid does well in the game, McMahon says, it is the parent who feels a surge in self-worth. But if the kid's team loses, the parents are crushed, defeated, and depressed. They are the ones who feel like failures. Says McMahon, "We have to put a mirror up to the culture and ask is this the best we can offer our kids and ourselves."

I interviewed kids who say they worry what their parents will think if they get a B instead of straight A's. Sarah, seventeen, regularly turns down weekend recreational activities in order to study, write papers, and practice ballet (which has become a chore, but which she continues for the sake of her college application and her parent's approval). Sarah tells me, "I guess I do feel like things are better with my parents when I get good grades. And my dad definitely wants me to go to a better school than he went to."

Moms who are busy pushing their kids with agendas for success or falling prey to crazy societal expectations can lose all sense of the big picture. When a mom's sense of worth depends on her child's getting the starring role in the school play or scoring goals on an elite soccer team, it's time to step back and ask, *What do I really care about? What are my long-term goals?* When the anxiety gets so overwhelming that a mom loses sleep when her kid gets passed over for the advanced orchestra, there's something out of whack, and it's hurting both kids and parents.

### Changing Competitive Culture

John Yokoyama, owner of the World Famous Pike Place Fish Market in Seattle, understands the harm that can come from creating a competitive culture. When he opened his business, his sole purpose was to sell fish and pull in a sizable profit. When he first started his market, he viewed his staff as faceless objects whose only function was to achieve his agenda for success, which was profit, period. Employee theft, high staff turnover, and rampant drug use threatened to put him out of business. He made several mistakes common to a competitive culture: he failed to find ways to infuse meaning into his employees' daily toil; he imposed his agenda, treating his employees as commodities; he failed to get to know his staff as people; and he refused to provide them with meaningful input into the daily workings of his market. He was so busy striving for his version of success that he lost all sense of joy and fun—and so did his staff.

How did he turn his business into the most profitable fish business in the country? He saw that employee morale was in the toilet and that there was increasing criminality in the workplace. So he did a very smart thing. He changed the culture. He altered his purpose: instead of striving only to increase profits, he sought to make a difference in the lives of his employees and customers. By changing his definition of success and tapping into the interests, ideas, and passions of his employees, he enlisted his staff in his vision to create a world-famous fish market based on employee individuality, humor, joy, and an athletic sense of reckless abandon that truly reflects the culture of his now famous market. He is wildly profitable and has a waiting list of employees eager to join in the fun.

Changing your definition of success can have dramatic results at home as well. When the measure of success shifts from getting straight A's to tapping into your child's passions and creativity, you achieve what many mothers say they want for their child: a sense of meaning and fulfillment and a love of learning. There are three primary strategies to turn a competitive culture around.

**1. Discover Their Passion** Listen with curiosity for areas that inspire your kid's enthusiasm. Michael Morgan, the conductor of the Oakland Youth Orchestra, cautions parents against imposing music on their kids if they don't show a passion for it. "You can watch kids go about their day and find what excites them. Is it building Legos, turning somersaults, dancing, writing? Music is not for every kid," says Michael.

This advice comes from a man who lives and breathes music and embraces a personal mission to turn youth on to music every day.

At a workshop on parent leadership, Karen shared that her daughter was spending her time stuffing backpacks with blankets and socks for the homeless, a worthy enough project, but not when it started getting in the way of her doing well in school. Karen was worried. She feared that her daughter was putting obstacles in her way that she couldn't see now but that she'd later regret—obstacles that would keep her from getting into a good college. I asked Karen to share what her primary purpose was as a parent, the goal she had shared at the beginning of the session. She found the piece of paper where she had written her purpose and read it to the class: "To raise a compassionate daughter who follows her faith and does good in the world."

The entire class gasped. Karen cried. With this little epiphany, Karen could relax, ease up on the power struggle, and realize that her daughter's actions were tightly aligned with Karen's primary goal. She began to feel pride, an emotion she had bypassed on her way straight to worry.

Julie Reinganum, forty-nine, wants her daughter, Maya, nine, to pursue her own passions. Athletic herself, Julie would love Maya to play soccer, but Maya isn't interested, and she gets to decide. "There are all these ubiquitous activities that everyone does—piano, soccer—and Maya isn't interested. But she likes sewing. I can't stand sewing—but that's what she likes," explains Julie. Julie exposes Maya to some activities that are nonnegotiable: Sunday school and Chinese class. But she gives Maya freedom to choose her other activities and tries not to let her own agenda distract Maya from her own interests.

Great parents, like great leaders, provide guidance and instill values, but they don't expect others to be versions of themselves. They celebrate individuality and independence. The big-picture parenting goal here is to help your child discover his authentic self. Give yourself a high-five every time you do something that encourages your child to be himself, not a replica of you.

**2. *Pursue* Your Own *Dreams*** Thankfully, we've rejected the notion that children should be seen and not heard. But wait. Parents in some families, intent on elevating their children's status in the household, have themselves taken a dangerous demotion in status. They're so busy enriching their children, helping them discover *their* passions and maximize *their* potential, that they've neglected their own dreams. If you say "You can be anything you want to be" and then put your own life on hold, what are you telling your children?

It's also important to recognize when you're imposing your unlived dreams on your child. A friend of mine refused to let her son quit his tennis team. My friend had been a tennis star in high school until she injured her knee. Now she wanted her son to excel in the sport that she had found rewarding as a kid. Finally, she acquiesced and let her son quit when she recognized that her son's passion would never be tennis and that she was living her own unfinished dreams through her son. To all those soccer parents screaming on the sidelines: maybe it's time to put on your own cleats and take to the fields!

**3. *Encourage Mistakes***    I can't say this enough: you can't learn, grow, and succeed unless you experience failure. A little suffering is good. If you don't allow your child to take risks and at times stumble, he won't have the skills or confidence necessary to survive life's setbacks. Failing a test, getting passed over for a school play, struggling with a new sport—all of this equips kids to cope with difficulty, learn from mistakes, and gain the confidence that comes from recovering after a failure.

Nancy Ortberg, a leadership consultant and the mother of two daughters, 19 and 15, and a son, 14, encourages people on work teams to see mistakes as opportunities to learn and grow. She tells a story about a manager at IBM who made a mistake that cost the company a lot of money. He went into his boss and said, "I suppose you want my resignation." The boss said, "Are you kidding? We just invested a bunch of money in you. Now you learn from your mistake and get back out there."

At home, Nancy feels less accepting of her own mistakes. "I've made so many mistakes. I can still remember when my son was five and he was yelling from the basement, 'Mom, Mom, come here!' Impatiently, I screamed back, 'What. What do you want? What?!' Finally, I walked down to the basement, where my son showed me a big sign he made that said 'I love you.'" From that moment, she decided to learn from her mistake and make a conscious effort to be more patient.

Nancy tries to bring home the lessons she teaches people at work. She recently took her oldest daughter, Laura, to college. She describes Laura as a perfectionist, hard on herself when she makes mistakes. Before she left her daughter in her dorm room, she gave her a mistake journal and told her,

"Write down three mistakes every day and realize that we still love you and tomorrow's another day. Don't just record small mistakes. Make good ones."

□□□

If you're like the rest of us, you'll no doubt find some trouble spots in your culture. Pick one or two areas on which you want to focus. Go back over the chapter and identify a couple specific activities you'd like to try or behaviors you'd like to change. It helps to write down your ideas and then land on a commitment or two that you will follow through on during the next several weeks. You may decide to encourage your child to do his own laundry, or maybe you are going to start that exercise routine to get more fit.

With a healthy culture, you are better equipped to weather the inevitable crises life can bring. In the chapter ahead, you will learn leadership strategies that can guide your business and your family through stresses and over hurdles. Inspiring stories demonstrate the essential practices that can keep your family and your children resilient through death, divorce, and other family crises.

# LEADERSHIP STRATEGY 5

# *Leading Through Crisis*

How do you recover from disaster? You do it by meeting it and going on. From each you learn something; from each you acquire additional strength and confidence in yourself to meet the next one when it comes.

—Eleanor Roosevelt

The most successful business leaders and family members can help people not only survive crises but also turn them into opportunities to grow. We have all met people who turn even the slightest of life's annoyances into supercharged calamities. Similarly, we know stoic, remote leaders who never let themselves be vulnerable. Even the best leaders struggle through dark periods and get overwhelmed; what makes them different is that whereas others get stuck and never move on, the most effective leaders find hope and rebound. So the question is this: How can we find ways to pull ourselves together even when we feel overcome with stress or grief, enabling us to provide strong leadership in the middle of a crisis and not turn it into a total disaster?

A crisis is a turning point: either we are left helpless and overwhelmed, or we find hope and, in many cases, grow stronger as a result. Why do some people thrive in crisis while others wallow in gloom? Why do some companies grow despite the fiercest competition while others crash and fold? In the heat of a crisis, good leaders embrace specific attitudes and behaviors that make all the difference. They employ leadership strategies that you can use at home and at work to build up your hardiness, enabling you to confront crisis with agility and to help others pull through with self-confidence.

## CHARACTERISTICS OF HARDY PEOPLE

We all know that some people are tougher and more resilient in crisis than others. Psychologists Suzanne Kobasa and Salvatore Maddi set out to discover what made the difference. They studied executives who endured high levels of sustained stress at work. They discovered that some individuals coped better—experiencing a lower incidence of illness and greeting turmoil with optimism—whereas others were overwhelmed by their challenges and fell ill. Kobasa and Maddi found that those who deal more effectively with stress and crises possess three major attributes: commitment, challenge, and personal control. They describe commitment as having a sense of purpose that gives meaning and passion to what we are doing. Instead of resorting to self-pity, the hardy individuals face adversity with a commitment to strengthen the lives of others. I don't want to create the impression that strong leaders never fall apart. They do. But they find the right time and safe outlets where they can lose it, knowing that they can't offer truly compassionate leadership unless they take a turn receiving compassion from others.

The second element, challenge, is about seeing the learning opportunities in hardship. The hardy executives confronted stressful situations head-on and searched for opportunities for learning and growth, whereas the others grew discouraged and pessimistic. Kobasa and Maddi found that the hardy executives became energized by their hardship and infected others with their optimism.

The third attribute, personal control, is displayed when individuals focus on areas where they have influence over the situation rather than feeling at the mercy of circumstances they can't change.

A lot of mothers I work with feel that they handle work crises better than crises at home. Of course, crises that affect your family are much more emotional, with higher personal stakes. Yet the techniques business leaders use to strengthen their resilience during a crisis can be brought back home.

### Hardiness in Action

Carol Evans, CEO of Working Mother Media, clearly demonstrated hardy leadership in the face of crisis. Carol realized a long-standing dream by acquiring *Working Mother* magazine in 2001, but a mere three weeks later, the terrorist attack on the World Trade Center took place. Not only were the employees of the magazine emotionally devastated, but the advertising industry came to a standstill. Suddenly her dream was teetering on the brink of demise.

For the next year, she and her team worked day and night for the magazine's survival. Carol took some strong measures to keep the magazine afloat. She cut the circulation of the magazine back by 19 percent and reduced the staff to a core group. She closed down business units that weren't profitable, and implemented expense controls.

Carol involved as many people as possible in her decisions. She kept in touch with her investor group, brought in an executive coach to work with her management teams, and held an offsite meeting with the heads of every department to establish a clear mission statement for the new company—To Serve Women Boldly—that would guide them for years. And she relied on the expert knowledge of people in the industry to guide her work with major customers.

"Behind the scenes, I was deeply concerned, but in public I needed to convince everyone that we were strong and we were not just going to survive, but that we would thrive," said Carol.

## Bringing Crisis Management Home

Carol is, no doubt, well equipped to face problems at work, but in her home, she feels it's much more difficult. Carol has two children, Robert, twenty-one, and Julia Rose, eighteen. Between the two, she has had to face a number of crises, and she admits to feeling a lot less powerful at home than on the job. "The stakes are so high," she said. "You can and will recover from a crisis at work, but when something happens to your child, your whole world falls apart." That's why we can't afford to leave the best of our leadership skills at the office.

Carol used her leadership skills during a number of childhood crises. Her son, Robert, was born premature and had hydrocephalus, for which he needed surgery when he was eleven months old. He has been challenged academically with a serious learning disability that took years to diagnose and manage.

But Carol's toughest test came just after her daughter turned seventeen. Carol noticed that Julia's eating habits had changed and that she was losing weight. But she had no idea that Julia had fallen victim to a terrible eating disorder. She learned the truth when she got a call from her daughter's pediatrician saying that Julia's weight loss was dangerous and that she would have to be admitted to the hospital immediately.

That was the beginning of a terrible, dark time. Julia was admitted to the hospital to stabilize her heart. From there she entered an inpatient clinic, Renfrew Center, near Philadelphia, where she stayed for six weeks. She then went to outpatient treatment and slowly began to get control over Ed, the name that anorexics call their disease.

"It was incredibly difficult," Carol told me when we talked about this family crisis. "I didn't know anything about anorexia. At first I thought we would beat this problem in a week or two of therapy. But as I learned more I realized my optimism was actually getting in the way of my ability to plan realistically for Julia's needs. Finally, a therapist at Renfrew told me that it could take three years before Julia completely recovered. That was a turning point for me. After I got over the shock of that timeline, I realized I had to take a whole new approach to this problem, and engage a completely different set of skills."

What Carol did was to begin a long-term plan for her daughter's recovery. And she asked for help—from her coworkers, her family, the therapists, and her executive coach. With this team on board, Carol was able to become much more involved in her daughter's recovery. She traveled twice a week to Philadelphia to attend the family therapy that Renfrew was famous for. She leaned on the magazine's president, a working mom herself, to take on more so that she could focus on her essential work tasks and her daughter. She relied on her executive coach to think through strategies both for work and for supporting Julia. She allowed herself to talk about what was really happening to Julia, and she took support from her customers, friends, family, and management team. Taking these steps allowed Carol to stay strong in the face of her fear, to focus on helping Julia get results from therapy and treatment, and to keep on an even keel by getting help for herself so that she could help Julia.

Through it all, Carol embodied the three characteristics of the hardy executive. She demonstrated *commitment* by facing the facts and staying focused on the highest priorities. She faced the *challenge* by remaining optimistic and inspiring confidence that everything would be OK. And she demonstrated *personal control* by focusing on what she could influence, taking the actions needed to weather the crisis as successfully as possible.

As Carol's was, your job as a mom in crisis is to take swift action in areas where you have control, stay connected, face the realities of the crisis without losing sight of your big-picture goal, divide the problem into manageable steps, and stay hopeful. When confronted with a menacing situation, you won't always know the best course of action. Even the strongest leaders feel scared as they negotiate new and treacherous territory. The key to surviving crisis and even thriving is to learn all you can as you go, stay optimistic, and get back on course when you make a mistake.

While learning as much as she could about the hard-to-beat eating disorder, Carol focused on what she could control. She put her busy CEO tasks aside as much as possible and spent hours knitting with Julia and playing Scrabble, Scattergories, and Taboo with her; Julia welcomed the connection and the distraction. Like that of many mothers who go through crises with their children, Carol's connection with her daughter deepened.

## FOSTERING YOUR OWN RESILIENCE

Not everyone can exhibit the characteristics of a hardy personality in a crisis, but the good news is that everyone has the capacity to be more resilient. How do you boost your resilience? Here are some strategies to strengthen your hardiness and display hardy leadership when crisis hits:

- **Clarify your highest purpose.** With their desired result clearly in sight, leaders focus on what they can control in order to move them closer to their goals. Without a compelling purpose, you are tossed about by the forces of change without any focal point to help you stay on course. What is your overriding passion? Do you want to promote greater self-confidence in your child? What professional goal gives your life meaning? John Yokoyama, owner of Seattle's World Famous Pike Place Fish Market, whom we discussed in Leadership Strategy 4, transformed his business on the verge of bankruptcy with a newfound, gripping purpose: to make a positive difference every day in the lives of each of his customers, suppliers, and colleagues.

- **Convene your support team.** When you're enduring a crisis, you need people you can trust. Make sure you seek out people who are not caught up in the crisis, who can help you regain perspective when you're in the thick of it. Who are those people who believe in your ability to get through a hard time, even when you lack that belief yourself? Whom do you know who steps up to help and maintains a healthy, positive attitude even in the face of misfortune? These are the people to reach out to during challenging times.

- **Prioritize the crisis into small and manageable steps.** Focus on what you have control over and leave the forces outside your influence alone. Identify the most important first step. Carol had to find a new revenue stream to revive her company. She launched its conference business. Her daughter was in the hospital. Without knowing the exact cause of her condition or how to cure it, Carol knew she had to give her daughter the support of her presence, 24/7, and moved into the hospital to be with her. Once you take that first step, you're ready to figure out your next move. The point is to keep moving strategically forward toward your desired outcome. Find those actions that yield quick, high-impact results.

- **Transform crisis into opportunity.** Reframe a negative situation to reveal the possibilities that might, in time, materialize. A professor of mine once told a little story about a shoe factory that sent two men to scout out a region of Africa to study the prospects for expanding business. One of the men sent a telegram back to the head of the factory saying, *Situation hopeless. No one wears shoes.* The other man wrote back, *Glorious business opportunities. They have no shoes.* Many crises have hidden possibilities if you adopt the right state of mind.

## FOSTERING RESILIENCE IN OTHERS

It's not enough to build up your own resilience. What about promoting resilience in people you work with and, most important, your partner and children?

One thing you can realize as a parent is the value of allowing your child to experience difficulty. The struggle in today's over-protective society is to allow our children to confront life's challenges without intervening. In fact, it is our job to *unprotect* our children at times so that they develop their resilience muscles.

I'm not talking about throwing your toddler into the deep end of the pool; but by allowing your children a reasonable amount of discomfort and then helping them manage the resulting distress, you are supporting a valuable long-range objective—to raise resilient children who can cope effectively with life's inevitable pain.

According to my own experience and to research by leading resilience experts Robert Brooks of Harvard University, Julius Segal of the National Institute of Mental Health, and Bonnie Benard of the nonprofit research agency WestEd, you can foster resilience in others—your kids or coworkers—by demonstrating five key leadership traits:

1. **Develop caring connections.** Display kindness, empathy, and compassion.
2. **Create motivating conditions.** Show your faith and help people shift from discouragement to optimism.
3. **Empower people.** Find creative ways to involve people and to help them express themselves and have meaningful input.
4. **Set an example.** Model resilience when you confront challenges.
5. **Focus on the big picture.** Make choices that support your overriding goal—for example, to promote self-confidence, even at the expense of more immediate concerns about your child's discomfort.

Debbie Bonzell, a training specialist, displayed these five leadership traits when her fourteen-year-old son, Zackary, was punched in the face at his middle school and came home bloody and bruised. He was minding his own business, walking from one class to the next in the busy hallways, when a boy in a hooded jacket smashed his fist into Zack's face and ran.

Debbie was outraged, not to mention scared and worried. Knowing that Zack is a self-confident kid, she held herself back from swooping in and demanding justice. In fact, she did just the opposite. She let him know—through her words and actions—that she believed in him and was confident that he could navigate through this difficult situation.

Zack made it clear that he didn't want his parents to make a big deal about it at home or at school. So instead of raising a ruckus, Debbie and her husband kept close watch and discussed with him ways they could make the school safer while still respecting Zack's wishes to stay low key.

They all met with the administrator of the school to talk about ideas to increase security during passing periods. They encouraged the school to hire more security guards to keep close watch in the school's breezeways. They worked together every step of the way to figure out how to influence change at the school, but at the same time they respected Zack's middle school instincts to avoid bringing unwelcome attention to the incident. Zack convinced his parents that he was fine; he felt safe enough to quickly return to school and was ready to move on.

But when a second act of violence occurred the following school year and Zack was slammed up against a locker until a teacher came and pulled the other kid off, Debbie's anxiety soared. Although her initial instinct was to swoop in and snatch her boy from harm's way, she again calmed down by focusing on her big-picture goal—to equip Zack with the self-reliance to handle adversity. She monitored the situation, asking Zack for hallway reports and asking lots of open-ended questions about whether he was jostled or messed with at school. Debbie and Zack had regular follow-up conversations. She and her husband attended meetings at the school about how to increase safety. If Zack had been freaked out and traumatized himself, then Debbie and her husband would definitely have pondered pulling him out of the school. But given Zack's response, she felt strongly that to take more aggressive action would have caused more harm than good. She kept in mind that Zack was watching her, learning how to react in the throes of difficulty. What good leaders know is that their behavior forms the ideas their followers will have of

---

## ARE YOU AN OPTIMIST OR A PESSIMIST?

Think of a challenge you are currently confronting.

1. Can you see anything positive that might come out of this situation?

2. Are you taking action to influence the outcome?

3. Do you see the light at the end of the tunnel?

4. Do you see this situation as a limited piece within the context of a good life?

5. Do you recognize and appreciate the valuable lessons that came out of past difficulties?

6. Can you see what strengths you gained as a result of personal or professional hardships?

7. Do you engage in any activities that improve your mood, such as exercise or reaching out to friends?

---

In reality, most people fall along a continuum of optimism to pessimism. Even those who usually see the glass as half full experience their bleak, soul-draining struggles. Even the most optimistic leaders don't flip a switch when they get discouraged and suddenly become optimistic. There is usually a messy process in between that involves soul searching, falling apart, and getting support. With this caveat, if you answered yes to most or all of the questions here, you probably tend toward an optimistic view of the world and have a strong sense of self-efficacy. Where you answered no, you might want to consider ways you can gain control over your situation:

- Find the opportunity in the challenge.
- Identify where you have influence over the situation.
- Divide the problem into more manageable steps.
- Think about the positive aspects of your life.
- Think about how you got through challenging situations in the past and how they made you stronger.
- Most important, commit to reaching out for support and engaging in self-nurturing activities.

how to regard difficulty. If you fall into self-pity or paranoia, or become paralyzed with anxiety, they will follow suit.

At the end of the day, Debbie focused on what she could influence: how Zack thinks and acts.

"I didn't want to be the Norma Rae of the school, knowing there was only so much I could control. I wanted to be the Norma Rae for Zack and influence how he thought about the situation in a positive way," said Debbie. They strategized how Zack could better defend himself; he needed to keep his eyes on his surroundings, steer clear of certain kids, and stay with groups of friends. Zack didn't start carrying Mace or thinking paranoid thoughts that more bad things might happen. Thanks to his parents' positive attitude, he just chalked it up to once again being in the wrong place at the wrong time, and bounced back.

What if Debbie had followed the instincts that kept her awake at night and pulled Zack from the school he loved? She mulled and fretted over options with her husband, but stayed upbeat about the school with her son, knowing she could easily imbue in her son a fear that would only undermine his confidence.

Zack witnessed plenty of other acts of violence at his school, but he took the high road, continuing to participate in enjoyable activities—the school's jazz band, a baseball team, and his church youth group. He was never hit again, and graduated from school with the highest academic honors.

"Zack never showed signs of fear, but my younger son, Casey, did in anticipation of going to Zack's school when he reached middle school age," said Debbie. She helped Casey quell his fears by pointing out the randomness of the incidents. She focused her son's attention on how much Zack loved his school, his friends, and his teachers. Zack's enthusiasm about his school, unspoiled by the violence, filled his younger brother with positive excitement and anticipation about entering the same middle school the following year. Debbie is convinced that Zack's experience, after the initial setback, increased her children's self-assurance.

## EMOTIONAL INTELLIGENCE

One key to being an effective leader during a crisis is a hefty dose of emotional intelligence. If you look closely at the strong leadership at the helm in any crisis, you're likely to see the four components of emotional intelligence deftly displayed. The first two competencies focus on self-awareness, the second two on awareness of others.

**1. Self-awareness** is the ability to read your mood and be clear about what you're feeling. If you have strong self-awareness, you are clear about what you are feeling, which helps you stay in control when high emotions threaten to take over and cloud your good judgment.

We all have blind spots that keep us from seeing our strengths and weaknesses accurately. I've watched countless leaders with glaring blind spots who instigate crises through their lack of self-awareness. The boss whose unruly rebellions against her staff create a chilling effect throughout the office is in the same category as the mother who is oblivious that she's creating tension throughout the house when she's in a bad mood.

In their book, *Primal Leadership: Realizing the Power of Emotional Intelligence*, Richard Boyatzis, Daniel Goleman, and Annie McKee describe how accurate self-assessment correlates with superior performance. Among the several hundred people they studied from twelve different organizations, the best managers had just as many shortcomings as those with inferior performance or productivity, but they were aware of them and could therefore take responsibility for their weaknesses and improve, whereas the less successful managers lacked this self-awareness. From self-awareness springs the ability to correct shortcomings and recognize the role we play in interpersonal situations.

**2. Self-regulation** is the ability to see anger or a bad mood coming on and control it or explain the source to others so that they don't take it personally.

We all have war stories of falling victim to someone who lacks impulse control. I still cringe when I think about a boss early in my career who yelled at us for the smallest offenses—a messy desk, a typo in a memo, a late arrival at a meeting. To give you a sense of how unpleasant she was, I celebrated when I learned that I had to have an ovarian cyst removed, requiring that I take one glorious, boss-free month off from work.

Maintaining self-control despite agitated customers, whining toddlers, a crabby husband, or disgruntled teenagers (as we'll explore in the next chapter) proves to make a world of difference in the success of your relationships with others. Let's be realistic: sometimes you might face adversity that knocks you down and sets off your most primitive emotions, but good leaders get the support they need to climb out and reregulate their emotions.

Self-regulating doesn't mean imploding. Holding your feelings inside not only creates health problems but also often indicates an unwillingness to express feelings in a way that improves the situation. Expressing anger and sadness can help resolve conflicts, set an example for open communication, and teach emotional intelligence, whereas stifling feelings can block an important source of connection. The trick is to show self-restraint while staying emotionally respectful, open, and expressive.

**3. Social awareness** is the ability to exercise empathy and political acumen. If you possess this competency, you can navigate office politics and group dynamics and show sensitivity to the impact of your relationships on others.

Building a strong team that encourages mutual respect and cooperation is a key task for a business leader, family member, or parent. Bringing social awareness to work or into the home can promote esprit de corps. But a lack of social awareness—sadly more common in the work teams I see—leads to fragmentation, divisiveness, and apathy. Leaders with strong social awareness have teams or families who

- Respect and trust one another
- Communicate openly and honestly
- Have fun together
- Cooperate and share responsibility for common goals
- Appreciate each other's strengths and accomplishments

**4. Relationship management** entails de-escalating conflicts, displaying compassion, and building nurturing relationships.

Few of us have these emotional sensitivities on autopilot. But remember: whether you are acting as a mom or a boss, your behavior is contagious. If Mom is happy, everyone's happy.

If Mom is moody and cranky, the feeling will infect the entire family.

People with good relationship skills listen well, take cues as to when to intervene and when to step back, understand others' point of view, and provide meaningful support to people in need.

Focusing exclusively on relationships can backfire, however, especially during a crisis. Take the leader who wants to be liked: she may overidentify with others and bend over backwards to accommodate their needs, but fail to make the hard decisions that may be unpopular in the short run but that are ultimately for the greater good of the organization.

Maintaining your emotional intelligence and sensitivity is difficult when you're working with people who are angry and distrusting—especially if these feelings are a reaction to an unpopular decision you made. Sam Schuchat, director of California's Coastal Conservancy, had to keep his agency afloat in the midst of turbulent times. When he assumed his position as the agency's new leader, he had to make some hard decisions, including laying off more than thirty people—not exactly the way to endear himself to his new staff. After announcing the inevitable layoffs, he was referred to as the "Angel of Death."

Sam knew that his credibility was on the line. The way he guided his remaining staff would either foster bitterness or renew commitment. How would he repair relationships and resurrect his reputation and his agency?

Sam had to use his emotional intelligence. He knew he had to be patient and regain people's trust—if he were to make unilateral decisions prematurely, even if he was sure they would ultimately benefit the organization, he would meet with resistance. But he also felt a sense of urgency. His first priority was to build back his team. He had to read people's moods, remain calm, empathize, show humility but also confidence, diffuse conflicts, and build relationships with people who were anything but receptive.

"I knew I had to act like I knew where we were going even if I wasn't always sure," said Sam. He told his staff that if they pulled together, they could create a thriving organization.

In meeting after meeting, Sam stayed confident that the organization would survive—and thrive. "Like a patient who survives heart disease, with a strong new heart we will have good times ahead," he told them. Gradually, people's uncertainty about their future and their doubts about Sam subsided, and they began to get down to the business of constructing a successful organization. By engaging people about how to best move forward; respecting people's messy feelings, from outbursts of anger to debilitating apathy; and bolstering confidence with a hopeful message about the future, Sam led his employees across a chasm from despair to optimism. Soon he was able to engage his staff in problem solving and decision making. He formed committees of staff and board members and assigned research projects to employees to make them a part of the process.

Sam didn't have a clear plan for how to revitalize his fledgling organization, but he had the self-awareness and relationship management skills to create a trusting, cohesive team. Now he oversees a flourishing organization that has helped preserve almost two hundred thousand acres of wetlands, wildlife habitat, recreational lands, and farmland.

But things were tougher for Sam at home. His daughter, Rebecca, was dead set against a decision he and his wife made to enroll her in a new middle school. Rebecca felt as if her parents were ripping her from her all-important friendships. From her point of view, to leave the school she had attended since kindergarten, where the majority of her friends would continue to go without her, was a crisis of huge proportion.

Anytime that Sam or his wife suggested that things would work out all right, Rebecca rolled her eyes and stormed out of the room. Sam realized that he had to use the same tools at home that he'd used at work. So he acknowledged his daughter's feelings and reassured her that they were normal and that he had confidence in her ability to make new friends. He engaged Rebecca in figuring out ways to ensure that she would stay connected with her old friends, and shared stories about how he stayed connected with his old friends from various schools he had attended. It took a hefty amount of creativity to find ways to connect and to move past the sulking and tears. Sam found good times to talk—in the car, at bedtime, and (his favorite) on a chair lift at their favorite ski resort. Eventually, Rebecca came to love her new school and found ways to stay close to her old friends.

## LEADING CHILDREN THROUGH ILLNESS AND DEATH

The most difficult situation for a parent, of course, is when a family member's health or life is at risk. How does a parent lead when the most basic security in a child's life is threatened?

Sophie, a management consultant, demonstrated powerful leadership even in the face of serious illness. Her husband, Josh, was diagnosed with colon cancer with a prognosis of 10 to 15 percent chance of survival when their daughters, Simone and Erin, were seven and four. Sophie suddenly understood the truth behind stories of parents lifting cars in emergencies. Her guiding purpose—to preserve her daughters' carefree childhood despite this life-altering crisis—gave her a strength she didn't know she had. Like Carol, Sophie put her emotions aside when reassuring her daughters.

"I was forced to stay present. I didn't want to rob them of their lives," said Sophie. She says that Simone and Erin helped her and her husband remember that they had to hold it together. The girls compelled them to be wacky and silly, to find pleasure in the present, and to take lots of vacations together. Everyone in the family pulled together to do things they would remember, in order to create good memories. When Josh's cancer recurred, he and Sophie had the grandparents take the girls to a dude ranch while they consulted with doctors at the Mayo Clinic.

During the course of Josh's illness, Sophie, previously introverted and private, had to reach out and accept the favors of friends and neighbors. She felt humiliated and exposed, but appreciated the stability that her community provided. Her support team represented a much-needed silver lining, giving the family an enduring lesson about the power of generosity and love. They experienced the best of human nature. When

---

## BUILD YOUR SUPPORT TEAM

A strong web of relationships is a powerful shock absorber for the stress that crises bring on. Talking with close friends and colleagues is the best way to find meaning, soothe your emotions, and understand your reactions. Friends can not only provide practical support but also validate your emotions and help you uncover the positive underneath the emotional chaos.

Write down a list of people you can depend on. You might want two separate lists, one with professional colleagues with whom you can talk about work, and another with personal friends.

What can you do to bolster your relationship with people on the list?

Whom would you like to add to your list?

What actions are you willing to take to add this person to your list?

If you don't already have a mentor, think about a leader whom you admire and whose behavior you emulate. Seek this person out and get closer to him or her. People are usually flattered and willing to help.

Sophie felt as if she were in danger of falling off a cliff, it was this support that kept her feet on the ground. They received an anonymous check for $1,500 from her husband's work. Neighbors cleaned their bathrooms and fixed their dinners.

Today, with grown children and a cancer-free husband, Sophie remembers the lessons she learned from those tumultuous years. The entire family learned to pass on the generosity they received to others in need.

## How Much Information Do You Share?

When crisis hits, you need to determine how much of what's going on you plan to share. Carol Evans didn't share all the ins and outs of the magazine's budget with the entire staff. She shared what they needed to know, and emphasized the good news in order to be reassuring. Likewise, Sophie's message to her daughters was, "You will be OK, you will have a good life, and you are loved." She made a strategic decision that many friends and professionals advised against. She didn't tell her kids the whole truth—Josh and Sophie didn't use the word *cancer*. They felt it would needlessly frighten their daughters. Sophie drew pictures of the tumor and talked about the doctors who were well trained to cut out the bad cells and make Daddy healthy again.

Clearly Sophie was not conniving or dishonest. Rather, she was guided by what she considered a higher value—to protect her children's right to a happy childhood—instead of sticking to the one value of honesty. Of course, such information can't always be under strict control. Sophie's plan worked just fine until a friend at school asked Simone if her dad had cancer. That evening when Simone came home and asked her about it, Sophie was able to respond that, yes, her father had cancer, but that the doctors had taken out the tumor and were working hard to get rid of all the bad cells—and at this point Simone was able to hear it.

Here are some helpful questions to ask when deciding how much information to share. Would the information

- Reduce fear and anxiety?
- Support a deeper purpose—for example, to protect a child's quality of life?
- Minimize surprises for which people need to prepare, depending on their age?
- Build connection?
- Foster hope?

## Suffering Makes You Stronger

Crisis itself makes you stronger. Bonnie Benard, the resilience researcher, asked thousands of people what fostered their resilience. Their answer: adversity and challenge. "They learned they could indeed mend stronger at the break."

Lynn Lazurus, a family physician and mother of two, helps people through suffering every day. But that didn't prepare her and her husband, Andrew, for the dilemma they faced when their son's best friend, David, four years old, was diagnosed with terminal cancer. Lynn's first impulse was to protect her child from suffering. But on reflection, she found that a deeper purpose—to teach a valuable lesson about friendship—emerged.

Lynn watched as some other parents were pulling their children away from friendship with David because they thought it was too painful for their own kids. Lynn and Andrew knew that the situation might destroy a small part of their son Sam's childhood. But the two children were best friends and had known each other since they were eighteen months old. Like Sophie, Lynn was guided by a conscious decision to discover and follow her deepest ideal, which in this case was to teach her son that when someone you love gets sick, you take care of him. Both Sophie and Lynn went counter to what others advised. They carefully considered what others advised them to do, but ultimately trusted their own instincts and made a bold choice, inspired by their deepest values.

"We knew staying close to David might be sad for our child, but hopefully it would teach him the most valuable lesson: if you have a friend in dire need, you care for him no matter what happens," said Lynn. Lynn and Andrew held on to this deeper principle as David grew sicker and eventually died. They gave their son the support he needed, reassuring him that his sadness was perfectly normal and that his pain would eventually ease with the help of all the fun memories he had with his best friend.

Leadership is not about shielding people from hardship, but about managing the resulting distress that follows inevitable challenge. Carol Evans, Sophie, and Lynn Lazurus employed two key tactics to help people through hard times: they validated and supported people's feelings as normal and expressed confidence that those feelings wouldn't last forever. People who cope best see their adversity as temporary. Lynn told her son that it was normal to feel scared and sad and reassured him that he would eventually feel better.

These two messages are important for anyone to remember in challenging situations big and small: your feelings are normal and I'm here to help you with them, and you won't feel this scared and sad forever.

Lynn told Sam that his friend had a sickness that he couldn't catch and that was so rare that he may never know anyone in his life again who had it. Lynn watched Sam for signs of distress as he continued to want to play with David until his dying day. As she did with her patients at work, Lynn told Sam that David would die eventually, unfortunately, so that Sam could prepare.

Lynn also performed decisive acts of leadership in her community. David's parents were both out of work when their son was diagnosed. She figured out the most urgent priority: to raise money to pay for David's health care. As David got sicker, she and other parents started a foundation, and they raised $130,000.

"There were moments when I wanted to pull away, but I reminded myself of the most important value, and that transcended my urge to back off," said Lynn.

Several years later, Sam said, "I'm weird. No one I know has lost their best friend."

"That's OK. You're special, and you have done a wonderful thing," Lynn told her son.

Lynn, taking into consideration the temperament of her son, determined the appropriate level of protection Sam needed while exposing him to a valuable life lesson. She was there to provide support and instill in him a deep value about love and friendship that eclipsed the suffering he endured.

---

## DISCOVER YOUR HIGHER PURPOSE

Reflect on a challenge you have recently faced or are currently facing. Identify the best thing that could come out of this crisis *in the long run.*

What will success look like several years from now?

What lessons will have been learned?

What sacrifices might occur in the short term if you make choices that support your higher purpose and long view?

What eventual greater gains will override these sacrifices?

Write down your purpose and keep this readily available as a reminder to shape your choices and attitude.

## Building Confidence from Crisis

Crisis made Lynn Bravewomon and her fourteen-year-old son stronger and more confident. When Sam, then eleven, sliced his hand clear through the muscle with his new knife on Christmas morning, Lynn had to put her queasiness aside and show up as a strong leader. Struggling to stave off her rising panic, she managed to remain relatively calm to assuage her son's fear.

As they went through the emergency room triage, Sam was getting more panicked, and Lynn struggled to hold back her own anxiety. "I let him know I was there to help him through it even though I was feeling panicked too. I stayed calm enough to tell him that rather than shutting down and abandoning himself in the process, he could unabashedly express his fears too. I knew if he could stay present, he could learn from this and grow stronger," said Lynn. He got his injections and stitches, stayed fairly calm, and realized he could get through it.

Humor helped. As the doctor stitched him up, he told Sam he'd been called every name in the book. He told him that Sam's most important jobs were to keep breathing without passing out and to hold completely still, and that if it would make Sam feel better, he could feel free to call the doctor any name in the book and he'd buy him an ice cream if Sam called out a name he'd never heard.

After another couple of anesthetic injections, Sam started getting overwhelmed. Lynn was freaking out watching her son losing it, so she engaged in the game. "I said to Sam this hurts so much that if I was eleven, this is the name I'd call the doctor . . . ," rattling off a few crude words.

After the stitching was over, they were proud of each other knowing how well they handled the situation, given that they both tend to lose control in bloody situations. Lynn told her son that they together did something that neither of them thought they could do, that they had conjured up the courage and did it. Sam's fear of hurting himself diminished after that misfortune. Both Sam and Lynn did indeed grow stronger at the break.

# DIVORCE

My parents divorced when I was twelve. When my father broke the news to me, I remember two main reactions. First, I was relieved: no more dreading when my father came home and a deep freeze enveloped our house. Second, I was scared: Would this mean moving from my house, my friends, and my school? Would we still go on vacations? How would we make it money-wise on my mom's schoolteacher salary? Would I live with my mom? Would I have to spend more time alone with my dad, a frightful thought? I believe these are the kinds of questions most kids have when their parents decide to divorce. Some others that I recall: Where will Dad live? Can I still go to camp this summer? Can I still be on my softball team? Was the divorce my fault? Would I still get the ski jacket my mom told me I could buy?

Yep, I really did worry about that ski jacket with the yellow and orange stripes across the back (and did get it, to my relief), which points to the seemingly trivial things your child may find important. You won't know their concerns unless you carve out lots of time for talking.

There are plenty of great books out there that suggest age-appropriate ways to break the news, describe common psychological reactions, and offer best practices. It's not true that divorce automatically ruins a child's life forever, as some pundits would have it. But no matter how it's handled, divorce disrupts children's lives. Only by exercising good leadership tactics can you keep the damage to a minimum and improve the odds that positive outcomes will result from the challenge of divorce.

## Focus on the Big Picture

When Dana's eleven-year-old daughter said at the dinner table, "Daddy treats you worse than Uncle Vernon treats Harry Potter," Dana knew she had to leave the marriage. She realized that she was putting up with disrespectful behavior from her husband that she would never want her daughter to endure now or in any adult relationships. After going through years of counseling to no avail, Dana finally concluded that the dynamics would not improve.

Dana didn't want to teach her daughter and younger son to repress their feelings or submit to abusive behaviors from anyone. She realized that the dynamics of her marriage ran counter to the values she was teaching her children. Consequently, her ambivalence about whether to stay or leave eased, and she made the hard decision to divorce.

## Set an Example

Divorce is hard. Staying in a bad marriage can be worse, especially for the children.

"I knew I had to forge a different path. I needed to be my own role model so I could set a positive example for my kids," said Dana.

The good news is that divorce provides the opportunity to show how adults can respect and cooperate with each other. For some divorcing parents, modeling strong relationship skills is easier once they decide to separate. If you and your former partner can maintain a civil relationship and work as a coleaders of your family with the best interests of your children at heart, you can continue to be positive role models. For me, watching my parents fight every day was far worse than coping with their break-up. When they both eventually remarried, I had the good fortune to see my parents happy and to see what a good marriage looked like.

## Connect and Support

As in any difficult situation, the most important antidote to crisis is a caring connection. In the case of divorce, this means supporting your child even when she acts out. For one dad I know, there were plenty of days when he looked forward to picking up his five-year-old daughter from school, only to be greeted by "I wish you were dead so I could just live with Mom."

Although heartbroken to hear this, he simply said, "I don't blame you for being angry at me because our family is no longer together as it used to be." His daughter's comments were hard to hear, but he knew that she needed to have the intensity of her feelings acknowledged and heard. Effective parents and leaders aren't superhuman. They have their own messy feelings, but they know when they need to remain composed and when they need to seek solace from trusted confidants and express their own vulnerabilities and complicated feelings. All good leaders need a place to blow off steam so that they can be there for others.

I routinely give my clients the following advice for dealing with upset employees: listen and validate, validate, and validate some more. The same advice holds true for separating or divorcing parents. You can only try to make the situation easier, but in the end, you can't fix it anyway. One manager, after listening to his upset staff express their resentment about their company's relocation plans (which he knew he couldn't fix), said, "I know you're unhappy we're moving our headquarters to Sacramento. I understand how upset you are and that you really wish we could stay here. I know that for many of you this means a much longer commute." Your job is to be a good listener, even when it's difficult to hear what people have to say. This manager couldn't change an unpopular decision, but by listening and empathizing, he was able to ease some of the anxiety.

Just like good bosses who encourage employees to bring problems to their attention, good parents encourage children to feel comfortable sharing their troubles, and let them know that someone is there to listen and support them. Sometimes children need a little prompting to share their fears. Clinical psychologist Susan Greene, Ph.D., says that 95 percent of children think it's their fault when their parents divorce. "They may not ask because they don't want their fears confirmed," says Dr. Greene.

It's important to tell children often that the divorce had nothing to do with them.

You can't guide your child through the stormy seas of divorce when you are drowning in a whirlpool of anger and emotion. It is difficult enough to be a good role model and convey optimism when you are going through emotional upheaval, but it is impossible when you are constantly fighting with the other parent. Even though divorcing parents may know intellectually that their child will bounce back, it's hard not to react in the moment when she displays regressive behavior like bed wetting or thumb sucking, or says "I wish you were dead." Parents going through divorce need to seek out caring connections, whether with family, friends, or therapists, in order to "be there" in an appropriate way for their child. This is a time when it truly takes a village or at least a few stalwart villagers to help you through so that you can help your child through as well.

## Coleadership During Divorce

As if divorce weren't painful enough, you need to develop a strong sense of being on a team with your ex-spouse, of all people. During and right after divorce you may be angry, hurt, or devastated, so your ex is the last person on earth you would want on your team. But child psychologists advise parents to think of the long-term needs of their children and work together for their best interests.

Child psychologist Barbara Waterman, Ph.D., says, "The most important predictor of how kids fare post divorce is the ability of the parents, even if they hate each other, to work together to support the needs of the children." Putting your child's needs first is easier said than done. Dr. Greene says that most parents who come into her office embrace the idea of putting kids first, but their actions can contradict their good intentions. For example, divorced parents with joint custody can have a tough time adjusting to spending less time with their child.

Parents may put their own needs first, not realizing that they are overlooking their child's needs. Eager to spend their "shift" with their child, they discount that their child may, for example, want to spend her time at a birthday party with friends.

"I often hear divorced parents argue about 'your time' versus 'my time,' forgetting that it's the kid's time," says Dr. Greene. It's important to remember that good leadership relies on putting the best interests of others first.

I often coach leaders at work who don't get along well with a coleader or team member. As is true in families, the rift is felt throughout the organization and takes the form of divided loyalty, anxiety, and confusion. I advise business leaders to fortify their relationship skills for the benefit of their "followers."

The same goes for parents: watch for trigger points for both you and your ex so that you can better regulate your emotions and keep a check on hostile behavior, especially when your children may be listening. For your child to be able to remain a child amid the turmoil of divorce, it's important to resist pulling him into disagreements. If you and your ex work out solutions together and show a united front, your child will not be put in the position of choosing sides.

Laura Garcia-Moreno, a literature professor, knew that her sixteen-year-old daughter, Ines, was facing a difficult decision. Laura's ex-husband, Ignacio, asked Ines to stay with him for a semester when he was a visiting professor in Norway. With their bitter divorce still painful even after six years, Laura's knee-jerk response was a flat-out "no way." She was furious with her ex-husband for even suggesting that Ines move halfway around the world from her, so she resolved to pull legal rank if she was forced. Very soon, though, she realized that taking this hard-line stance would be a big mistake. Ines could hold it against her, and Laura didn't want to put her daughter in the position of choosing sides. Another important consideration was that the trip might prove to be a once-in-a-lifetime opportunity for Ines. Like all great leaders faced with a tough decision, Laura knew that her own needs must be sacrificed so that her daughter would benefit.

At first, Ines decided she didn't want to leave her mother or her friends. Laura made it clear to Ines that she didn't want her to go, but also made it clear that her sadness at being separated from Ines was a separate issue and that Laura would support whatever decision she made. Laura told Ines that she would be happy for her and that although she would miss her terribly, their connection would remain strong and grow in new ways. Laura decided to put her own embittered feelings about her ex-husband aside and collaborated with Ignacio to figure out what was best for Ines. Together they decided to empower Ines by allowing her to make the decision herself; whatever she elected to do would be fine with both parents.

When Ines was stuck in indecision and her deadline to register for her upcoming school semester was fast approaching, she turned to her mother for advice, but Laura knew she couldn't make the decision for her daughter. In fact, she worried that if she influenced the decision, she might interfere with a great opportunity for her daughter to experience another culture and establish a positive connection with her father. Even if Ines's visit didn't go well, Laura was confident that her daughter would learn something valuable.

"I told Ines that neither I nor her father could tell her what to do. This was her decision. I didn't want to influence her decision, even though I felt strongly that I didn't want her to go. I worked hard to set aside my emotions about Ines and my negative feelings about my ex-husband."

Laura made an important decision. Realizing that neither she nor her ex-husband could offer their daughter neutral counsel even though they both expressed their support for whatever she opted to do, Laura suggested that Ines talk to the school counselor, which she did. After her first meeting with the counselor, Ines realized that she did indeed want to go to Norway.

In the end, Ines had a fabulous time making Norwegian friends, gaining confidence in a foreign culture, and learning to speak

Norwegian. Most important, she returned home with a greater sense of self-confidence and a faith in her own power and judgment. Ines and her parents were thrilled she had had the opportunity to spend part of her junior year of high school in Norway.

In the workplace and at home, coleaders set the tone of the environment. Henry Koltys, a family law mediator and attorney who developed KidsFirst!, software that helps parents collaborate after separation, sees a direct parallel between sound management practices and reaching resolution in custody disputes.

"Taking a cue from leaders who must often manage divergent interests and motivations, parents who separate must realize they will continue to share mutual interests, so should learn how to cooperate and collaborate," says Henry.

As in the business world, where great leaders must put aside their personal agendas and keep sight of the bigger goal—in this case, the child's best interest—divorcing spouses must also rise above their strong feelings to reach common ground.

You have a precious opportunity to teach others about the realities of human relationships. Although we won't want to work with everyone and we won't always get along, we can still show respect for others, cooperate to achieve common goals, and resolve disagreements with civility and even kindness.

## Opportunities for Involvement

We all want to feel in control over our life. Divorce represents a startling departure from the status quo, with unfortunate consequences forced on the child by others. When anyone, adult or child, is denied the opportunity to control his or her circumstances, the outcome is often anger and sometimes outright despair. In the workplace, I often see unilateral decisions that negatively affect people, and the resulting consequences are usually sabotage, apathy, and sometimes rebellion. Likewise, a child with a compromised sense of power and control over her own life can give in to unhealthy impulses, including and especially turning anger on herself or her parents. The more that parents provide opportunities for the child to participate and to regain control over a decision that disrupts her life, the more likely it is that parents can avoid or alleviate a child's depression or anxiety.

Just as great leaders find innovative ways to engage their team, parents should seek out creative ways to involve children and to give them a voice, enabling them to feel heard and understood. To smooth the transition, keep schedules as constant and transparent as possible and inform your child about his routine and about decisions that affect him. Involve your child in writing his schedule on the calendar to track when he is with Mommy or Daddy and to record upcoming activities. Carve out time to discuss ideas for fun weekend or after-school activities. This sounds so simple, but if your child understands his routines and feels that he has a say in how he'll spend his time, he can begin to heal and feel more in charge of his life. The more that children feel in control of their family life, the more they can regain a sense of security.

□□□

All the leadership strategies that strengthen families during hard times will be needed for the gargantuan task of parenting teenagers. Many parents I talk to call adolescence a crisis. Sex, drugs, rebellion, eating disorders, hormonal swings—parenting teenagers takes every last bit of hardiness we can eke out plus an entirely new set of skills. These skills are similar to those required when dealing with disgruntled employees, except for the small detail that you can't fire your children or fall back on your formal authority over them.

The next chapter doesn't offer any easy, cookie-cutter solutions to parenting children during the turbulent teenage years, but you will be heartened to learn that you're not alone and that there are leadership strategies that can help you feel more in charge and less, as one mom described, as if you were tone deaf and mute and had two left hands.

# LEADERSHIP STRATEGY 6

# *Managing the Growing Pains of Adolescence*

If you lose connection, you lose everything.

—Joe Di Prisco, coauthor of *Field Guide to the American Teenager*

A perfect parent is a person with excellent child-rearing theories and no actual children.

—Dave Barry

I recently told a client that my thirteen-year-old daughter was having her Bat Mitzvah ceremony in a few weeks. She said, "Enjoy her now, because it's the beginning of the end. My daughter's Bat Mitzvah wasn't about becoming an adult, but the beginning of her transition from a kind, happy girl to an alien."

That wasn't the first time I heard a dire warning of what's to come for a family with one or more teenagers. When I told another mother how I couldn't imagine that my daughter would go through that kind of horror movie transformation, she looked at me patronizingly, exasperated by my naïveté.

"Just wait until high school," she said. "That's when all hell breaks loose."

I hoped not. In fact, I was so determined to prove them wrong that I went on a mission, talking to hundreds of parents about whether they shared this negative view of teendom—and if they did, what to do about it.

## THREE KINDS OF FAMILIES WITH ADOLESCENTS

What I found out is that most parents of teenagers are indeed frustrated with their kids. Beth Goldberg, a management consultant and mother of Maya, sixteen, and Ari, thirteen, describes parenting a teenager as a "blood sport." She told me—as many other mothers have shared—that after so many years of feeling like a good mom, these days she feels completely incompetent.

"At home, I feel idiotic, like I speak another language," she says. Her battles at home take far more dexterity—and energy—than even her toughest situations at work. "In consulting, there's a puzzle to solve, and I am given the robe of authority, a contractual arrangement where people want my assistance," she says. "You find data, hypothesize, and strategize. It's cerebral. But with teenagers, it's more emotional, and more primitive."

Other moms told me how challenging—and painful—it can be to have sullen teenagers in the house. "This kid that once clung to you lovingly, now says 'You smell, you're ugly, I hope you know how much I hate you,'" one mother told me.

"It's hard to take." As one mom explained, "Even for the most thick-skinned parent, nothing prepares you for the disdain of a teenager."

Despite stories like these, I found out that some parents struggle more than others, and not everyone buys into the dire predictions about teenagers. The parents I talked to can be roughly divided into three camps.

The first group rejected the teenagers-are-hell point of view, and were happy to share that their teenagers are still affectionate, saying "I love you" every day. (I'm not making this up!) Many parents in this group noticed that their teens were far more attached to their peers and more moody, but they described their kids as generally nice people to be around. Most of them, it is interesting to note, added that all was well . . . *so far*, acknowledging that they too had heard the worst and were bracing themselves for the possibility of rough seas ahead.

The second group comprised parents whose teenagers struggled with drug use, sex, volatile moods, and eating disorders, but who still felt close to their child, were determined not to give up, and continued to be the child's ally and trusted her despite her sometimes poor choices.

The third group of parents had simply given up, describing their kids as perplexing and maddening, and declaring the situation hopeless. One mom in this camp said, "I throw up my hands. My son is going to do what he wants no matter what I say, so I'm going to ride it out and hope for the best." Another said, "I'm going to ride out this phase and hope my son returns to earth someday soon." There's a great *New Yorker* cartoon that depicts a dad in this camp: the father says to his adolescent son, "Young man, go to your room and stay there until your cerebral cortex matures."

I realized that of these three groups, the first two would reap the benefits of staying engaged and continuing to believe in their child. The group who gave up would have a more difficult few years ahead. But what will help those who throw up their hands and give up is asserting leadership even if their teen responds with defiance during this challenging period.

## THE IMPORTANCE OF
## TRANSFORMATIONAL LEADERSHIP

Transformational leadership requires that we lift others into their higher selves. This is especially important to keep in mind during your child's adolescence. Giving up signifies a failure of leadership. Whereas a boss's best option with a perpetually insubordinate employee may be to fire him, a parent doesn't have that option. The leadership challenge for you as a parent is to find ways to begin to reconnect with your child and your long-range parenting goals.

Remember that your kids are dealing with a barrage of challenges too. As our teenagers teeter between childhood and adulthood, their hormones surge and their bodies and brains change. Meanwhile, they have to navigate a deluge of temptations, from sex to drugs; negotiate pressures from peers, school, and parents; and deal with their self-esteem in the context of sexualized messages and images in advertising, on TV, and on the Internet. So it's no wonder teenagers often exercise poor judgment.

Everything you've read up to now—that your task as a leader at home requires focusing on your big-picture goals, setting an example, establishing clear expectations, listening, trusting, and connecting—holds even more true when raising a teenager. You need agile leadership to guide this transformation from child to adult in all its glory and chaos. You have to be flexible. Often the strategies that worked well when your child was younger have to be tossed out in favor of a new mindset and set of skills.

Fortunately for us, our kids' independence emerges gradually— this process began years ago when they went off to all-day kindergarten, summer day camps, and sleepover camps. But there's a point when most parents experience the door-in-the-face epiphany and realize that their clingy, doting, ego-gratifying child is gone. This is a trying time for families and requires your most nimble leadership. Your authority goes up in smoke. What you have left is influence.

Your degree of influence depends on your ability to sustain your teenager's self-worth, preserve a trusting connection, and ease up on the control. Business leaders who have the most positive influence are more willing to give up control and allow people to fully participate in decisions that affect them. They trust people and, in turn, get trust back. The same goes for you and your teenager. The tricky part is figuring out when to give up control and when to pull parental rank. When your teenager defies your authority and stays out an hour past the curfew you set, when you find a marijuana pipe in your son's underwear drawer, when your daughter refuses to come to the dinner table, your first impulse—to assert control—may be exactly right. But how you blend control with listening and trusting makes the difference, as we'll see in the strategies ahead.

How do you exercise your authority while still providing the freedom your child needs to grow into a self-confident, mature adult? You have to use solidly anchored transformational leadership, the kind of leadership that shows sensitivity to people's needs (in the case of the teen, the need for more autonomy and your unwavering trust) and in doing so inspires people to reach their full potential. You may not see this "higher self" emerge during the teenage years; in fact, research by scientists at the National Institute of Mental Health found that the part of the teen brain responsible for judgment and self-control is still under construction, and therefore your teen's recklessness may be blamed on an undeveloped frontal cortex. But according to brain researchers, this neurological fact doesn't justify your merely riding out the teen years. Helping your teen exercise good judgment and self-control lays neural foundations that can "hard-wire" your child for success. Now there's an incentive to hone your transformational leadership skills!

## EXPECT THE BEST TO BRING OUT THE BEST

To understand how to manage the teenage years, let's go back to the workplace, where we've all experienced how leadership can bring out the best—or the worst—in others. In organizations where people feel that their ideas are valued and their talents are celebrated, and where relationships are built on mutual respect and trust, you can bet that they have a better chance for a successful future when challenges hit. More often, I work in broken organizations where management sees its role as that of policy enforcer and performance monitor, which is far less effective.

Companies, like parents, can build their transformational leadership skills, even under the most trying circumstances. At the Merced Human Services Agency (HSA) in California, I witnessed a spectacular transformation from a divisive, demoralized culture with high turnover to a collaborative, productive place where people liked to work. But it took a lot of effort from everyone in HSA.

## Turning a Rebellious Relationship Upside Down

When I first arrived, I interviewed managers and staff. I asked the twelve members of the management team to describe the employees at their agency, and I recorded their words on a flip-chart: irresponsible, lazy, lacking initiative, passive aggressive, and, as one manager put it, "If we give them an inch, they'll take a mile." (Bear in mind, there were hundreds of employees, all reduced to these negative stereotypes.)

I asked them why they thought the employees were so problematic, hoping they would take some responsibility. After all, they had hired them! All I heard was example after example of incompetence, justifying the managers' blame. Not one manager claimed to have any role in creating this good-for-nothing crew.

No surprise, HSA employees were similarly unhappy with their managers. They felt misunderstood and distrusted. As one worker said, "They expect the worst—so we give them the worst. I used to be hardworking, but I've realized nothing I do gets any recognition. They've turned us into a bunch of rebellious teens." There it was: *They've turned us into a bunch of rebellious teens.*

The reductive leadership tactics had the power to transform conscientious workers, many of whom came to the social service sector out of a desire to do meaningful work, into apathetic, defiant workers. The employees reduced their managers to caricatures as well. When I asked them to describe their bosses, they described them as controlling, distrusting, hypocritical, judging, critical, nagging, angry, punishing, no fun. Sound familiar, fellow parents?

Given certain conditions, people will respond predictably. If people feel their independence squelched, or if they feel that they don't matter, you've got a formula for big trouble. Likewise, if they're expected to perform poorly, they will live up to that expectation.

HSA's executive director, Grover O'Myer, realized that his agency was going nowhere fast. With his retirement approaching, he wanted to leave a positive legacy, preserving his own reputation and that of the organization where he had spent his entire adult life. He got to work.

Under Grover's leadership over the next few months, the agency went through an enormous change for the better. He turned the organization upside down, asking his employees, as well as the welfare clients they served, what *they* would do to make the organization better. He asked good questions, listened, and, most important, adopted their ideas—even suggestions that seemed outlandish. They opened satellite offices in remote areas where most of the welfare recipients lived so they no longer had to take long bus rides to the office in Merced, miles away from their homes. They set up help booths in the lobbies, arranged child care for welfare recipients, and partnered with local businesses to get people back to work. With the employees "in charge" and their ideas implemented, morale rose and the agency thrived. Staff who had been completely disengaged started taking on leadership roles. The place was humming with innovation within a matter of months.

## Closing the Gap at Home

Let's compare the dysfunction HSA confronted with common breakdowns that occur at home. The wide gap between management and staff struck me as similar to the gap between parents and teenagers. Recently I spoke to a parents-of-teenagers group at a church in an affluent neighborhood. I asked them to describe their teenagers. Here are the words they used to describe their children: lazy, moody, unpredictable, irresponsible, forgetful, selfish, thoughtless, unconfident, focused on peers, and dishonest.

Although I didn't have the opportunity to hear how their teenagers would describe these particular parents, I did poll other high school kids on another occasion. These were the most frequently mentioned words describing their parents: critical, overprotective, distrusting, controlling, nagging, moody, busy, clueless, naive, don't understand me.

You have the power to create environments at home and at work that bring out the best in human nature. People don't generally act out just for the fun of it; there are underlying causes. When you're exasperated by infuriating behavior, it's easier to label others than to look at yourself and how you might play into the problem.

Your job as a leader is to examine your own behavior and its impact on those around you. You'll have an easier time navigating the teenage years if you create a trusting climate at home. If your attitude is that your kid is a problem to fix, it's time to shift your mindset. *Your teenager is not a problem to be solved, but a person to be understood.* And with understanding comes the opportunity to influence.

Just like the employees at HSA who, when given respect and the power to provide meaningful input, became more engaged, young people hunger for respect and the power to influence their environments. In other words, both adults and children need to feel that they matter. According to a wide body of research, a youth's feeling of "connectedness," a sense of belonging to a trusting, respectful environment in which they grow up, is one of the most important factors in guarding against risky behavior and promoting psychological health. (We'll be further exploring the implications of connectedness in protecting against risky behavior.) If we embrace stereotypical views of teens as self-centered, irresponsible, and disengaged, we thwart our capacity to create the close connections necessary to support teens' healthy development.

## WHEN TEENS MESS UP

In order to be an effective, transformative leader, you have to believe in people. Trust is the cornerstone of influence. This is especially important to keep in mind when your kid messes up.

Obviously, the stakes are higher with your child than with your employee. You can fire an employee who performs poorly, but when your child misbehaves, it triggers anxiety that can cause you to overreact, wonder where you went wrong, or jump to worst-case scenarios. Your reactions to your child's behavior are different because the level of care is different, but the aims are the same: to foster potential and develop capability. Transformational leaders continue to have faith in people's abilities even after they make big mistakes, seeing their role as one of inspiring growth and helping people learn from setbacks.

I've heard parents of teenagers say they wish there were some kind of magic formula they could sprinkle on their teenagers to knock some sense into them. Well, that magic formula is your trust. When your child messes up, it's exactly the time you need to pour on that special elixir. Crisis provides the best opportunity to bond with your teen. Believe me: whether they show it or not, when they mess up, they feel the most vulnerable, embarrassed, scared, and worried. Your teenagers crave your approval—even at the time it's most difficult for you to believe that this is true.

Punishment, in contrast, is going to undermine your influence—and your potential for transformational leadership. Coming down hard with criticism and punishment ensures two things: your child will hide mistakes from you in the future, and you jeopardize his lingering self-confidence. But if you become his ally and convey your trust even when he has behaved irresponsibly, you can sleep well at night knowing that your child has learned that he has a safe place to turn when he gets in trouble: to you. If he knows you trust him, he'll believe he's a good kid even when he does something foolish and reckless. It is your job as a leader to bolster your teen's self-confidence and resurrect his sense of self-worth—*especially* when he makes a big mistake.

## Reacting with Love

When Jane Griswold's fifteen-year-old daughter, Heather, made a mistake she would undoubtedly remember for the rest of her life, Jane saw an opportunity to build her daughter's confidence and strengthen their already trusting relationship.

One night, Jane was awakened at 11:00. She walked down the stairs in her nightgown, expecting to greet her daughter, who was due home from a party. But when she opened the door, she was stunned to see the mother and father of a friend of Heather's, both of them uncharacteristically grim faced.

"We have Heather in the car. She's been drinking. We need to carry her in. She's unconscious."

They carried Heather to the couch, and Jane immediately called the doctor, who told her to bring Heather to the emergency room right away. After a long night of vomiting and moaning, Heather was physically OK, but suffering from a pounding headache, along with a colossal dose of embarrassment and shame.

Jane purposefully resisted interrogating her daughter or expressing disapproval of her poor judgment. She was plenty worried, angry, and confused, but she simply stayed close to her daughter, stroking her back and bringing her water and a light breakfast. She wondered if Heather's behavior had something to do with her grandmother's death just the week before.

When she was feeling a little better, Heather herself broached the topic of her drinking, saying to her mom, "I think my friends will forgive me, but I don't know if I'll forgive myself." She also said, "I'll never drink again." She immediately told Jane that she wanted to apologize to the parents who carried her out of the party and also to the parents who hosted the party.

Despite feeling unmoored by the whole situation, Jane could see that her daughter, a young girl who cared greatly about what people thought of her and who held high standards for herself, needed to be affirmed, her self-worth preserved despite the humiliation. Jane clearly stated that Heather had made a bad decision and that there would be consequences, but she wanted to give Heather the room to emerge from this situation whole, her dignity intact. She knew that her being judgmental about her daughter's misconduct would only make matters worse.

"I know Heather really well," she says. "I make it my job to know her—her strengths, weaknesses, her value system." Jane could see that her daughter was shamed beyond measure. Heather had passed out at the party, vomited, and wet her pants, and was carried out by two adults for whom she has tremendous respect. "My whole feeling was, I don't have to do anything. She is filled with shame and remorse—all the ingredients of a good lesson."

Jane was immediately impressed by the way Heather handled the situation: she expressed her desire to apologize to everyone involved, and she recognized that she had a problem for which she wanted to get professional help. She talked with her mother about how sad she had been the previous day about the death of her grandmother, and freely admitted that she had brought the alcohol to the party and that her drinking binge was completely premeditated.

Jane stepped in to offer assistance when Heather asked. Heather wanted to take flowers to the parents who carried her out of the party, but she didn't know what to say to them. Jane asked Heather how she felt.

"I'm embarrassed. I'm sad about Grandma dying," Heather said.

Jane said, "They want to see where your integrity is about this. Speak the truth."

Heather did. She brought the other parents flowers and looked at them in the eyes and apologized, explaining how upset she'd been about her grandmother's death. Later that day, Jane helped Heather strategize how to handle school the next day. They came up with a true and easy-to-explain story for the situation: I was having a hard time, I made a bad choice, I regret it.

Our job is to love our child whether she meets our expectations or makes a colossal mistake. Emmy Werner, a distinguished resilience researcher at UC Davis, wrote, "The resilient youngsters in our study (nearly 700 kids) all had at least one person in their lives who accepted them unconditionally."

## Seeking to Understand—Not Solve—the Problem

We would never wish experiences like Heather's on our children just so they could learn lessons, but as one parent whose daughter was at the party said, "Heather's experience was better than fifty lessons on the dangers of alcohol."

Heather's friends needed to process the situation too. They came over to her house the afternoon after the party and sat on the sunporch. Within moments, there wasn't a dry eye in the house. They shared how scared they were and that they had looked online about alcohol poisoning and what to do to help their friend. They wanted to cover for her, not get in trouble.

Jane's seeking to understand Heather led her to discover her daughter's struggles with depression. She was able to approach the problem by getting Heather the professional help she needed. Heather and her mom talked at length about her grandmother's death. They shared stories about her grandmother's life and cried together. Heather talked with her mom about how she had been feeling depressed even before her grandmother's death, a problem whose severity Jane hadn't been aware of. And Jane spoke about her own grief at the loss of her mother-in-law.

In the aftermath of Heather's visit to the emergency room, instead of becoming estranged, Heather and Jane deepened their connection. When your teenager shows poor judgment, you'll get far better results if you try to understand the underlying causes rather than merely to solve the immediate problem. Only then can you discover the kind of support your child really needs. Attacking the problem head-on may lead you to tighten curfews and impose restrictions, but at best you'll get cosmetic compliance—and, at worst, all-out defiance—while the root of the problem goes unaddressed.

## Setting Fair Consequences

After the dust settled, it was time to discuss consequences. Jane trusted that Heather would regulate her own behavior because she'd learned a powerful lesson. Heather, like most teenagers, has an inherent sense of what's right, and she knew she deserved some consequences for her misbehavior. I've heard many parents in my workshops complain that their own parents let them off too easy at times, and that they wish they'd had stricter guidance when they misbehaved. But if Jane had instituted a heavy punishment, she would surely have created undue stress and resentment, undermining her support for her daughter.

Jane took an appropriate course of action. She reviewed with Heather what she did that was dangerous and wrong, and together they created a consequence: for the next four weekends, no socializing with friends. Heather was actually relieved, glad to have a respite from the social pressures of her life. If your teen misbehaves big-time and you think, *I'm going to buckle down with tighter restrictions and curfews to get my kid to abstain from sex [or stop drinking or quit cheating]*, you're heading down a dead-end street. If he wants to engage in sex, drinking, and cheating, you can be sure he'll find a way. You'll be far more successful if you let go of any delusions of control and focus your energy on a worthy big-picture goal: to help your child resist self-destructive behavior by working together to set reasonable limits and consequences. A collaborative approach with a teen can build trust and connection even when the issue at hand is discipline for reckless behavior. All the resilience research suggests that the greater the care felt at home, the less teens are involved in risky behaviors, such as binge drinking, drug use, violence, and sexual activity.

Good discipline blends unconditional love with clear limits. Chris Hiroshima, chief academic officer of a city school district, remembers feeling like an ogre when her children were teenagers. She often felt that she was the only parent setting curfews and limits. Just as she did at work, she stood firm, believing that both employees and teenagers need clear parameters, clear expectations, and clear definitions of acceptable and unacceptable behavior. She saw a similar mistake in the workplace and in families: people waffled on asserting authority because it meant either losing popularity or confronting conflict. When leaders aren't in charge, there is chaos, and the family or employees operate without a rudder.

"I constantly have parents coming into my office with their kids who are having problems," says John Tannen, a high school English teacher at a public school in Delaware who won the district's Teacher of the Year award. He says that the worst kids, the ones who act out and get into lots of trouble, crave boundaries at home.

"One kid, Wes, told me what I've heard many other kids say: 'I don't want my mom to be my friend,'" says John. These kids push the limits at school and at home. They feel out of control with more power than they can handle. What they need most is guardrails—firm, fair, and consistent discipline. "It's amazing to me how well kids respond to nonnegotiables I establish in my classroom, as long as I help them see the worth of the rule—why it's important and fair," says John.

Effective disciplining means setting clear expectations ahead of time. If your kids don't fulfill the expectations you set, you reclarify your intentions and follow through on consequences. That's the basis of creating an accountable culture.

## Remembering Your Own Teen Experience

If you're still struggling to contain yourself when your kid displays high-risk behavior, try engaging in the humbling exercise of remembering the times you screwed up as a teen. How did your parents react? Did their reaction inspire you to do better next time, or did their response have the opposite effect?

Whatever the dynamic you grew up with, it's very helpful to remember that you were once an imperfect youth yourself, not to mention an adult with a full spectrum of human short-comings. When we get on our high horse, we forget our own imperfections. As Mike Riera and Joe Di Prisco write in their book *Right from Wrong: Instilling a Sense of Integrity in Your Child*, "Forgiveness is the daily bread of every family."

I remember when I gathered my nerve and hitchhiked with my friend Kathy when we were sixteen. Hitchhiking was under-standably my mom's bugaboo. She didn't have many rules, but hitchhiking was a big no-no. I clearly remember that as much as I enjoyed the esteem of the popular Kathy Smith, mostly I felt guilty that I was violating my mom's trust. I survived, but the guilt I felt, and my mom's unwavering high regard for me, gave me the internal voice I needed to quit after that first hitch-hiking experience. I think back on this with terror—what is my daughter Anna going to do to test the limits? I sure hope it's not hitchhiking! I want to believe that I will remember the power of my mother's trust in me—that even when I made a foolish mistake, it was my mom's unflappable belief in me that kept me on track.

## PROVIDE GUIDANCE WITHOUT MICROMANAGING

As a consultant, I'm at the top of my game when I work myself out of a job, providing guidance that people can adopt and then use independently. The same should be true for parents.

If when our kids reach adolescence we are still playing the caretaker role, we stand in the way of their self-sufficiency. Regardless of whether your teenager continues to depend on you for advice or rejects all manner of help, it's your task to make a job shift from caretaker to mentor in order to facilitate her autonomy.

The advice habit is a hard one to kick. I try to get managers to recognize that when they fall into the advice mode, their employees tune out or get angry. The same happens with teens, but usually more flagrantly because advice undermines their raison d'être—to gain independence from you. To accept your advice would be, in their eyes, one giant step backward on their road to individuating. You will get far better results if you guide people to their own conclusions by asking good questions.

## Making a Tough Decision

Joan resisted doling out advice to help her daughter, Erica, eighteen, navigate the vicissitudes of friendship. She and Erica had had a stormy few months, clashing over everything from curfews to piercings. But Joan vowed to disengage from the no-win power struggles and to experiment with stretching the limits of what she allowed Erica to do, regaining a huge amount of goodwill. Erica, Joan noticed, was lingering longer at the dinner table, laughing more, and closing her bedroom door less.

One afternoon, Erica came home from school in a particularly foul mood. To Joan's surprise, Erica not only shared what was wrong—that her close friend, Nora, had spent the day being mean and rude to Erica—but also did something she hadn't done in years: asked Joan for advice.

Nora had a big solo violin recital that night. Erica had promised to go, but after her friend's rude behavior, she didn't know if she should attend. Erica's friends advised her not to go, telling her that to go would be wimpy after Nora's mean treatment. Nora, they told her, didn't deserve Erica's friendship or attendance. One hour before the performance, Erica had a decision to make.

Joan was blown away that Nora wanted her opinion. "I didn't want to simply tell her what I thought—that when someone is that good of a friend, you allow them to be a jerk one day and remember the whole relationship and honor the whole friendship—so instead I wanted to somehow guide her to her own decision," Joan said. "She was so hurt that I figured if I doled out advice, she'd resist it anyway. If there was anything I'd learned at work, it was that if I took over and tried to fix the problem, it would backfire."

So Joan asked her daughter questions. Here's how it went.

Do you think Nora will admit she's wrong when you talk to her? *Probably.*

Why? *Because she's a good person.*

How will not going show her a lesson? *It will show Nora and other people that they can't treat me meanly and I'm not a wimp, that I'm strong.*

Do you want her as a friend into your future? *Yes yes yes.*

Do you really think standing there at the performance shows you as weak, or does it show you as someone who can see the big picture of your friendship? (*Silence*)

Erica decided to go to the performance. The minute she entered the auditorium, Nora ran up to hug her, thanking Erica for coming and apologizing, saying, "I don't know what got into me."

Erica came home after the performance and said to her mom, "How will I ever be as good a mom as you?" By trusting Erica to make a good decision on her own, Joan allowed her daughter to take responsibility for her decision and figure it out herself.

## Five Steps for Good Advice

When your teen approaches you for advice, here are five steps to keep in mind to help him learn problem-solving skills and develop self-efficacy—the ability to recognize the influence he has over events that affect his life.

1. **Express feelings.** Encourage your child to acknowledge what he's feeling: Is he confused, stressed, sad, angry? Ask him what he is most sad or angry about.

2. **Share your personal experiences.** When Nina Medford's son, Blake, came home distraught about his friend's rejecting him at school, she tried to comfort him until he blurted out, "What do you know? You've never had this kind of experience." His response made her realize she had never shared her own stories of facing similar difficulties or mastering comparable experiences. Sharing your stories about how you or family members faced adversity and got through it can have a powerful effect on a child's understanding of challenges. As we explored in the previous chapter, you have the opportunity to teach your child about how you face difficulty and transcend it.

3. **Identify a goal.** Ask him what he hopes will happen: What is his ideal outcome or goal?

4. **Find where your child has influence.** Help him think about where he has control over the situation. Guide him away from things he can't influence. If he wants to change how a friend feels about him, for example, gently guide him to think about what he can control and identify actions he can take to reach his desired outcome.

5. **Generate options.** Encourage him to think about a number of alternatives that will lead him closer to his desired outcome. Brainstorming a list of possibilities can be helpful. Talk about what he imagines might happen if he chooses various approaches, so that he can see the potential impact of his behavior—which options will likely make matters worse, escalate a conflict, hurt someone, or narrow the possibility of his reaching his desired outcome. Which choices will increase his odds of achieving his ideal result?

As you go through these steps, remember that you are your child's coach and advocate. Resist answering your own questions; let your child come up with his own ideas.

## TALKING ABOUT SEX

Many mothers are perplexed about how to talk with their sons and daughters about the emotionally charged topic of sex. Even though Temple University brain researcher Laurence Steinberg found that the parts of the brain that control impulses are still undeveloped, which may have an impact on teens' ability to understand or accept our messages about sex, the stakes are too high to resign ourselves to silently fretting. More than one million American teenagers get pregnant each year, and among sexually active people, teenagers have the highest rates of sexually transmitted diseases. The good news is that parents can have a strong influence on their teens' sexual behavior.

Teenagers are less likely to engage in early initiation of sexual intercourse when they have a warm, close relationship with their mothers, according to a study conducted by Robert Blum at the Center for Adolescent Health and Development at the University of Minnesota. On the basis of the results of the largest survey of teenagers ever conducted in the United States, Blum suggests that listening and respect increase the likelihood of a parent's words about sex having an impact.

Vanessa Van Petten, who at age seventeen wrote You're Grounded! to give advice to parents from a teen's perspective, explains that you can be the strictest parent in the world with the tightest curfews, and kids will still find a way to have sex if they want to. The real issue is to inspire teens to make wise, self-respecting choices.

When Vanessa was sixteen, she had a new boyfriend and contemplated becoming sexually active. Her mom knew that persuading her daughter to abstain from sex would have little impact. Instead, she talked to her about safe sex. What she said next, though a little shocking to Vanessa at the time, made a lasting impression, changing Vanessa's whole perspective of men. Vanessa's mom's credibility rose when she showed that she understood that teenage girls were not only sexually active

## TALKING TO YOUR TEENAGER ABOUT SEX

Here are some tips for how to talk to your child about sex, based on the research from the Center for Adolescent Health and Development at the University of Minnesota and on advice from Ivy Chen, "professor of sex" at San Francisco State University and UC Berkeley.

**Clearly express your values, but keep talks brief.** Instead of having a formal "sex talk," engage in conversations that are more natural and ongoing.

**Make fostering a warm, close, supportive relationship with your teen a high priority.** Studies that looked at more than five thousand adolescents and their mothers found a strong link between a close and positive mother-child connection and delays in the initiation of sexual intercourse.

**If you disapprove of your teen's engaging in sex, clearly explain why, emphasizing the importance of love and mutual respect.** Research found that teens whose mothers disapproved of their having sex were more likely to delay intercourse.

**Stay involved in your teen's day-to-day life.** Mothers who reported knowing the parents of their daughters' friends had daughters who were less likely to engage in sexual intercourse.

**Be aware of what's going on in your child's life.** In the study, 50 percent of parents whose children were sexually active were unaware of their sexual behavior.

The bottom line is to cultivate a respectful and trusting connection and convey that your child's health and self-respect are what's most important.

but also engaging in unreciprocated oral sex, servicing boys and then experiencing plunging self-esteem.

In a phone interview, Vanessa shared her mom's advice: "If you give your boyfriend pleasure, make sure it's equal—if you pleasure him, make sure he pleasures you. I realized my mom got it. At sixteen, oral sex was big for girls. For my boyfriend, it was all about getting sexual pleasure. He didn't respect me, so I broke up with him," Vanessa says.

Vanessa shared her mom's advice with her girlfriends, who also came to the realization that the one-sided sexual experiences they were having were unfair. Vanessa's mom appealed to her self-worth, and she didn't advise Vanessa to wait until she was in love, which would have fallen on deaf ears. She allowed Vanessa to draw her own conclusions based on a loving piece of advice: respect yourself. Whether you're talking with your teenager about sex, school, drugs, or their after-school activities, it all boils down to instilling self-respect in your teens and letting them know they have the voice and power to influence their environment and the people around them.

## WHEN TO EASE CONTROL AND WHEN TO INTERVENE

Tension will inevitably surface if you stifle your teenager's push for autonomy. The teenage years place a high demand on your capacity to step back and allow your child's independence to bloom.

### Stepping Back at Work

Steve Leonoudakis, a training specialist and father of two sons who are now in their twenties, learned the benefits in the workplace of stepping back and letting go of having to be right. He made impressive changes in his management style when he received some eye-opening feedback in a 360-degree evaluation process at his work. People perceived Steve as a controlling leader who always needed to be right. Although he had innovative ideas and was charismatic and dedicated, he wasn't getting the outcomes he wanted. People had shut down at his meetings or stopped showing up altogether.

Steve took the feedback to heart—that he was overcontrolling, overly invested in being right, too rigid about having people do things his way—and, after some soul searching, shifted his leadership style.

"I could see that the feedback hit the nail on the head," said Steve. He became a more collaborative, inclusive leader by keeping the same goals in mind but allowing people to achieve them in their own way. He let go of being right in favor of soliciting people's ideas and nurturing relationships by truly listening and being flexible to approaches different from his. He bit his tongue when the group came up with ideas that he flat-out disagreed with; in the long run, he discovered that goals were met, just not in a way he had imagined. Steve's less domineering, more yielding approach brought positive feedback. It took several months for people to trust the changes in Steve, but soon he was leading high-energy meetings without the passivity or push-back so characteristic of previous meetings.

## Stepping Back at Home

Despite his success at work, Steve's big challenge was transferring his new skills to home. Steve's younger son, Gabe, triggered his impatience.

Gabe was one of those kids who always wanted to live life fully, in the moment. As a high schooler, he did that by going surfing instead of doing his schoolwork. Steve worried about his son's future, badgering him about his "loser behavior" and hearing a predictable response: "Don't tell me how to run my life." When Steve got caught up in wanting to justify to his son how he was right, that Gabe needed to think more practically about his future, he lost the battle. If he was to make difference in Gabe's life, Steve had to make a conscious shift from being invested in being right to empathizing and strengthening the connection between him and his son. He noticed that if he shifted to the inclusive mode he had adopted at work so successfully, his son engaged with him. Bringing his work skills home, he dropped the need to get Gabe to do things his way, and let go of his futile attempts to convince his son to see life from his point of view. He saw both at work and at home that when he was pedantic, people tuned out. In contrast, if he asked his son or colleagues questions about their aspirations—what they enjoy, what matters most to them—he strengthened his connection and encountered fewer battles.

"When I resort to disapproval because my son's watching a DVD on the computer, which seems like a waste of time to me, he shines me on," Steve says. "When I celebrate his efforts and show true interest in his artwork, which is his passion, I'm being the kind of leader I hope to be."

Steve recognized a link that is important for us all to reflect on: when you dictate other people's behaviors, you get snubbed, blocking the results you're striving for. He could no sooner push his live-in-the-moment son to think more seriously about his future than hurry the forces of nature.

## Stepping in at Home

As damaging as meddling can be, there are times when stepping back is the wrong approach—when running interference is actually the best thing you can do, even when your kids resist your involvement.

Teenagers' use of the Internet is a good example of an area where parents need to be vigilant about setting limits, yet many parents take a hands-off approach, exposing kids to dangers that can have long-lasting effects. Just like businesses that aren't alert to external threats and as a result go bust, inattentive parents can inadvertently expose their children to such threats as cyberbullying and predatory sex offenders. Parents need to be on the ball about the perils of the Net and equip themselves and their children to stay safe.

Stories abound of digitally altered photographs of a person's head on a naked body passed around for everyone to see, mean-spirited gossip posted on MySpace, fake users who harass, or such sites as Juicy Campus designed to spread rumors. Teens post all sorts of compromising information and photographs, only to find out down the road that a potential employer has discovered them when they least expect it.

Parents have an obligation to show leadership by teaching children how to be responsible cybercitizens. Just as you would in the workplace, make agreements up front about how you will monitor computer use. If teens say you are invading their privacy, rest assured. Reading their diary violates their privacy, installing hidden cameras in their bedroom invades privacy, but the computer is public for all the world to see—including strangers, predators, and potential future employers. It's not a matter of distrusting your kids; it's about preventing the wild, untamed Internet from walking unaccompanied into your children's lives.

As one mom put it after her two kids stumbled upon a graphic video of a murder on YouTube and suffered from nightmares for months afterward, the Web brings the world into our houses, and it's our right and responsibility as parents to be gatekeepers controlling who enters our homes and influences our children.

## STRENGTHEN CONNECTIONS IN FAMILIES WITH TEENS

Connection can be difficult to sustain during the teenage years when your child spends far more time with her peers than with her family. Your teenager may come home from school and go straight to his room, slam his door, and lock it, but the important thing to remember is *don't give up*—even when you're on the brink of calling it quits.

There are tricks that you can keep in mind to connect with your teenager when everything she does pushes you further away. The key is to be creative, finding ways to make the most of fleeting times together. If you and your partner establish family rituals, such as eating meals together, long before adolescence, you set the stage for valuable payoff during the more volatile teenage years.

As Mike Riera writes in his book *Staying Connected to Your Teenager*, "when all is said and done, your connection is as strong a deterrent to drug and alcohol use as there is." When leaders build trust, others are more receptive and responsive to their positive influence.

Here are some ways to foster connection in your family.

## Family Dinners

You've no doubt heard about the unambiguous benefit of eating dinner together as a family. According to the National Center on Addiction and Substance Abuse at Columbia University (CASA), children who have regular family mealtimes at least three times a week are at a lower risk for suicidal thoughts, eating disorders and obesity, and substance abuse, and are more likely to be emotionally content, have positive peer relationships, and have healthier eating habits. CASA has found that family meals are the strongest predictor of academic achievement across race, gender, education, age of parents, income, or family size, and a stronger predictor of these outcomes than time spent in school, at church, playing sports, or studying. Those factors we examined in Leadership Strategy 5 that build resilience—connection, high expectations, and involvement—come into play around the dinner table.

The CASA researchers have found that one of the most important features of family dinners is telling stories. These stories, like those told in workplaces with strong cultures (see Leadership Strategy 4) create a shared history, a sense of belonging, security, and family identity. Children learn skills in the telling of stories: empathy, critical thinking, relationship building. A study at Emory University found that children who heard stories about their family's history—especially stories that demonstrate how people get through challenging experiences successfully—were more able to see themselves as having influence over events in their lives and had better chances of persevering through adversity.

---

## FIND YOUR OWN SUPPORT AND CONNECTION

Your child may offer only tiny windows of opportunity for connection. When you do finally catch a glimpse of your teen, he may tell you you're ugly. You need to find places for support and connection for yourself. Refer back to the box in Leadership Strategy 5, Build Your Support Team, for ideas to find people to cheer you on in the darker hours.

How often do you do something to rejuvenate yourself? When did you last confide in a friend about your teenager? Do you have someone to whom you can vent so that you don't lose your temper with your child? Whom do you know who is going through or has gone through parenting a teenager who could offer you a supportive ear?

Tina, mother of Marissa, seventeen, wishes in retrospect that she had sought more support during the hard years when her daughter contemplated boarding school, fought through the rigors of a competitive soccer team, and struggled with binge drinking. "It was a comfort to know I'm solid enough that she can push back on me and know I wouldn't fall apart or go away," says Tina. "She didn't have to take care of me, but I wish I had gotten more support for myself."

## Be Creative

When your kids seem impossible to reach, you need to start thinking about creative ways to connect with them. You can take a few lessons from workplace managers who've figured out new ways to improve their workplace culture.

Karen H., a human resources manager, learned the value of getting close to her employees when she started to hang out with her staff at lunchtime. She used to eat her lunch while working at her desk. One day she heard laughter in the break room and decided to check it out. At lunch, she heard some surprising comments from her employees that could have come out only in a safe, casual environment. From then on, she made a point of regularly eating with her employees. The result was a more engaged team, higher productivity, and better decisions.

"I learned more about my employees that day than I had in the five years I had worked there," says Karen. "We got to talking about changes in the department and personal things as well. I can't tell you how much I value that time." Now Karen's employees tell her how much they enjoy having regular access to her, having informal time to offer their ideas and bounce around concerns. The best leaders are out of their offices walking around and talking with people. They show their care by taking the time to ask how people are doing and to listen to them. Parents need to remember this important management tactic as well.

Rachel, a divorced mom of a teenage son, says she always makes a point of hanging out in the kitchen late at night. She gave up on trying to get her son to go to bed on time, realizing that his teenage body had its own rhythm. She turned this problem to her advantage by being available when the house was quiet and her son made his nightly voyage to the kitchen pantry for a snack.

Regan McMahon found two great ways to stay connected with her two teenage children. One was enjoying outdoor sports, such as baseball, swimming, surfing, hiking, skiing, ice skating, and kayaking, as a family. "There's just something wonderful about learning a sport with your kid." She says a parent is very often in the role of teacher, being so much better at a skill than a kid that the inequity defines the experience. "But being novices together is different," she says. "You can stumble and triumph together, and rehash it all the way home." Learning together puts the two of you on a level playing field.

Regan's other connection "technique" is just to drive around with her kids—and their friends. Regan noticed that a lot of the parents in her community complained that in high school, they no longer knew their child's friends. Regan found a way around this problem: she drives her kids around any chance she gets. "It's great because you can be a fly on the wall, listening in on their conversations. They forget you're there, and you get to hear them talking about all sorts of things," says Regan.

---

## KEEP YOUR EARS AND EYES OPEN

An essential to being an influential leader is really knowing your followers. Understanding and appreciating who they are allows leaders to connect and influence. How well do you know your teenager?

- What music does he listen to?
- Who is his closest friend?
- What TV shows does he watch?
- Who is his favorite teacher?
- What activities inspire the most enthusiasm?
- What do his friends like most about him?
- What books does he read?
- What Internet sites does he visit?
- What's posted on his Facebook page?

# HELP KIDS RESIST UNDESIRABLE SOCIAL INFLUENCES

Peer pressure is the big bugaboo for parents of teens. We all conform to some degree because we want to belong and be liked, and it's never more true than for teenagers (think about how important your friends' opinions were to you at that time!). Social psychologists refer to this as "normative conformity." Teenagers are especially susceptible to acting against their better judgment, afraid that if they don't do what their friends are doing, they will feel isolated or ridiculed—even if it's doing drugs, being mean to a more vulnerable kid, or wearing a fashion that you think looks ridiculous. Further, as we discussed earlier, teens' brain wiring may not yet be sufficiently developed for them to be able to make sound decisions. Guarding your teenager against social pressures is a challenge for sure, but if you stay engaged, there's plenty you can do.

Some pressures are relatively innocuous—what teens wear, what music they choose—but it's the pressures that bring out antisocial or dangerous behavior that have us parents losing sleep at night. Will your son get into a car with a drunk driver? Will he say yes when the marijuana pipe is passed his way? Will she engage in unwanted sex to avoid hurting a boy's feelings? Will your son cheat because all his friends cheat? It's perplexing to try to understand what you can do as a parent to guard against the forces of conformity.

## Helping Your Teen Resist Peer Pressure

The best antidote to negative peer pressure is to keep your bond with your child strong. One of the ways you can do this is for you yourself to resist the widespread negative perceptions about teens. If you hold negative assumptions about your teen—for example, that he is reckless, selfish, and irresponsible—you won't be inclined to respect your child or value his input. No different than employees at work, young people hunger for your respect.

Standing up to peer pressure takes strong leadership and a lot of courage. You can help your child prepare for situations in which she has to decide whether or not to resist the powerful social temptations offered by her friends by teaching self-respect and leadership. Here are some tips to help your child be true to herself and resist the negative aspects of peer pressure:

- Talk about how your teen can respond when her friend passes her a cigarette, her boyfriend asks her to have sex, or her drunk friend offers her a ride home.

- Discuss with your child what he feels about sex, drugs, and alcohol. Do a lot of listening. Try not to lecture or interrogate. Help your child clarify his position on these issues, warning of risks but refraining from imposing dogmatic views.

- Help your child trust her intuition. If something feels wrong or uncomfortable, tell her to honor that feeling and let it guide her actions.

- Praise your child for his honesty and encourage him when he stands up for his beliefs, even if they are different from yours.

- Share stories about your experiences. Do you remember times when you went along with the crowd? How did you feel later? Tell tales about times you've taken an unpopular stand at work or with friends and how rewarding it felt afterward.

- Help your child feel good about who she is—not in comparison to her friends or her siblings or you. Convey to your child that she is OK just the way she is.

- Set an example by demonstrating assertive and self-respecting behavior.

## Finding the Flow

Parents can help teenagers resist negative peer pressure and participating in risky behavior by helping them find activities that are challenging and meaningful. Research at CASA (mentioned earlier) revealed widespread boredom and disengagement among teenagers. The study suggests that boredom may come from an overemphasis on school testing, a sense of irrelevance in the school curriculum, and a lack of opportunity for meaningful participation in school. Bored teens should arouse concern because youth who are unengaged are less likely to feel school "connectedness," a factor that current research has found to buffer youth from all sorts of risks, including sexual behavior, drug use, violence, and dropping out of school. CASA found that bored teens are 50 percent more likely to engage in smoking, drinking, and illegal drug use.

Schools play an important role in combating boredom by providing opportunities for creative engagement, but parents can address the problem of disengagement as well. You can seek out opportunities for your teenager to experience "flow" activities. The experience of flow gives you a feeling of being fully immersed and energized, and it happens when your skills are optimally tapped—you are neither overly challenged and therefore anxious, nor underchallenged and bored. We've all heard about the advantages of team sports, playing an instrument, or doing a public service activity that provides enjoyment and builds self-confidence. Activities that give youth a sense of flow go far to combat the negative forces of boredom, thus protecting against a whole host of risk factors.

Claremont Graduate University professor Mihalyi Csikszentmihalyi conducted a longitudinal study of two hundred teenagers in the late 1980s to find out why some are able to persist in practicing a skill and developing their talents to the fullest while others give up. One of his principal findings, published in *Talented Teens: The Roots of Success and Failure*, was that the experience of flow was the strongest predictor of engagement and how far the student advanced in his or her talent. How can we as leaders and parents help people find flow experiences?

There are three main steps you can take to promote flow:

**1. Promote learning for learning's sake.** Parents do best to focus attention on the inherent joy of learning. The result—getting high test scores, winning the game—needs to be secondary. But even when as business leaders and parents we say we want to instill internal motivation and a joy of learning for learning's sake, we can still send contradictory messages by putting too much emphasis on soulless values, such as profits or grades. For example, teacher John Tannen meets with countless parents who come to see him when their child gets a low grade. Invariably, they want him to change it, worried that a poor grade will damage their child's chances of getting into a good college. He's concerned that parents are sending two dangerous messages: first, that grades are more important than learning, and second, that kids aren't allowed to fail and, when they do fall short, that their parents will swoop in a fix it for them.

"When students complain about the grade they receive, I ask them, 'Have you learned something by studying for the test? In other words, do you know more about yourself today than you did before?' And then I ask them, 'What entitles you to an A? If you put in more effort, if you give your all, I'm confident you can earn a higher grade,'" says John. When students complain that his class is hard, he asks them, "Do you want me to dumb it down? No way. I believe in you. I think you can achieve a high standard." He wants them to know that he values them enough to keep the challenge high.

**2. Watch for signs of boredom or anxiety.** It's the job of a leader to watch people for these signs. When your teenager resists stretching out of his comfort zone, you may need to gently prod him to try a new challenge. A leader must also watch for signs that too much pressure is taking its toll. The best leaders protect people by creating what Harvard psychiatrist Ronald Heifetz calls a "holding environment," regulating the pressure by turning up the heat so that people are challenged, but also knowing when to allow some steam to escape. Sometimes that means holding steady and having the emotional capacity to allow people to go through struggles and pain, communicating confidence that people can handle the pressure. Other times it means finding ways to guard against the pressures that are creating distress.

---

## ARE YOU IN THE FLOW?

Csikszentmihalyi identifies the following six factors that come into play when you are experiencing flow:

- Your goal feels achievable.
- The activity matches your skills and abilities and is neither too easy or too difficult.
- You find yourself concentrating and delving deeply into the activity without distraction for long periods of time.
- You lose a sense of time passing.
- You feel a sense of intrinsic motivation; in other words, you do the activity for the sheer pleasure of it.

What activities create a flow state for you? Consider ways you can promote flow activities for yourself, your staff, and your children.

**3. Encourage goal setting.** Leaders are responsible for helping people set meaningful and achievable goals. Talk to your child about your own goals and how you work toward them. Think about how you talk about your work or hobbies. Not all of us have jobs that give us a deep sense of satisfaction, but it is important to convey to your kids the aspects of your work that are enjoyable and meaningful.

Activities that generate the flow state are a welcome alternative to activities with short-lived rewards, such as compulsive shopping or substance abuse. When people have flow-state activities in their lives, they are less likely to engage in self-destructive behavior. Ideally, by the time your child is a teen, she is able to set her own goals and find activities that generate the flow state.

□□□

The teenager whose parents offer her unconditional love even when she acts irrationally is much more likely to emerge from adolescence with a strong sense of self-worth. Young people crave closeness and approval from their parents above all else, even if they wouldn't be caught dead admitting it. When relationships get strained, it's easy to erect walls and drive communication underground. If you keep in mind the tenets of transformational leadership—set an example, keep your big-picture goals in mind, motivate by establishing high expectations, empower by allowing plenty of room for autonomy, and build strong connection—you have far greater chances of success during the tumult of adolescence and into adulthood.

You may be fully aware of the characteristics of transformational leadership, but how in the world do you perform as an exemplary leader day in and day out when the demands on your time just about kill you? The next chapter examines the so-called balancing act. Is there such a thing as balance for the working mother? We'll look at the lives of mothers who try to keep all the balls in the air. You'll learn techniques to help you keep ahead of the torrent of demands on your time, but we'll also acknowledge that you really can't do it all without some cost—to you, your career, and your family. The challenge is to minimize those costs and maximize the joy and fulfillment that are yours to enjoy as a working mother.

# LEADERSHIP STRATEGY 7

# *Balancing Priorities*

If your success is not on your own terms, if it looks good to the world but does not feel good in your heart, it is not success at all.

—Anna Quindlen

Manage time wisely at home . . . hmmm, herding cats or juggling flaming donuts would be simpler.

—Trudi Roth, mom and marketing executive

Our lives can get so busy that we acclimate to stress and neglect our needs until we fall apart. Having a satisfying career *and* a fulfilling life outside work *and* meaningful involvement in your child's life may just be an unrealistic expectation. Every working mother I know is flummoxed by the conundrum of doing it all without feeling completely spent by the end of the day. I don't know even one parent who wonders what all the fretting about work-family balance is about. Trying to have it all comes at a cost for sure, but there are things you can do (short of getting the United States to be more like Sweden and pitch in with support that families desperately need) to find more moments of fulfillment and spend less time on the verge of falling to pieces.

It's important to discover what success means to you. To do this you must quiet the expectations of others and trust your instincts—especially challenging when the treadmill reaches an unrelenting pace. Here is the key: how you spend your time must be a conscious decision that fits your authentic needs. Ignoring your inner voice can have a devastating impact.

Joan Barnes knows the hazards of trying to do it all. Founder and former CEO of Gymboree and the mother of two daughters, she worked night and day to build a business that provided children with a creative play environment while giving isolated mothers a social outlet. After a decade of hard work, her company grew to five hundred franchises and thirty-five retail outlets, with about $35 million in annual profits. She was cheered on by investors and colleagues, who told her she was a rare entrepreneur brimming with talent. Joan knew she was in over her head and had reached her limit, but she forged ahead anyway, caught up in the company's rapid rise from a small homemade venture that grew to a publicly held national business a few years after her breakdown. To handle the pressure, she hauled her employees in for aerobics classes that she led, and became a mountain biking "addict." She looked successful on the outside, but inside she was in agony, barely able to function. Finally, at the peak of "success," she suffered a full-blown nervous breakdown and had to surrender. She was also struggling with a long battle with bulimia that finally tipped her over the edge.

"I pretended that this was all OK," she says. "I didn't listen to my inner voice. I had one foot on the tightrope, with concrete under me. I knew my life was way too precarious, but I didn't know what to do about it."

Joan finally realized that she had no choice but to leave her family and Gymboree, and checked herself into an eating disorder treatment center. Her thirty-day stay turned into a one-year residence and five years of treatment away from her husband and her two daughters, one in college and the other in high school.

"I was completely broken down. I lost my marriage, my home, and my business," says Joan.

It took her five years to recover and gradually rebuild her sense of self. Joan learned to spend a little time every day in nature and alone, to listen deeply to herself. She started a nonprofit, Begin from Within, for people with eating disorders, and opened several yoga studios. Now, nearly two decades after she left Gymboree and still an avid entrepreneur, she enjoys close relationships with both of her daughters, Meegan, thirty-four, and Cecily, thirty-three. She finds that her yoga business combines her entrepreneurial skills and love of yoga to create a balance that keeps her energized and happy.

Clearly, Joan's struggle included many complicating factors that led to extreme consequences. But it is also clear that living a life so out of balance prevented Joan from recognizing that she needed to pull back from the precipice to prevent this hard fall. There is no one-size-fits-all formula for staying in balance. For some it means working part-time; for others it means launching a business. The point is that you have to listen to your own voice, know there are costs and trade-offs, and take care of yourself when you feel out of control.

## KNOW YOUR LIMITS

How do you know when you've hit your limit? When you're frantically racing from one task to the next, you can easily ignore your internal state until you realize you're unhappy and stretched way too thin to have anything left to give to your work, your family, or yourself.

Lian Dolan, author of Satellite Sisters' *Uncommon Senses;* cofounder of Satellite Sisters, a women's media company that creates content for radio and online; and mother of two boys, Colin, ten, and Brookes, thirteen, needed to take a hard look at what she had to give up, even when she wanted to do it all. Her show with her four sisters went to six days a week, and she was writing a column for *Working Mother* magazine, speaking all over the country, and touring with Oprah Winfrey. She and her sisters finally attained what for so long had been their dream, but for Lian these were the most dismal twelve months of her life.

"I absolutely couldn't say no to these business opportunities; it was all coming together for us. But at the same time, I was overcommitted at the children's school—on the board, chairing Grandparents Day, running the book fair—then a family member was diagnosed with cancer, and that was the tipping point. I was overwhelmed," said Lian.

Lian faced a typical paradox: when you're constantly busy, you don't have the energy to assess your priorities and figure out what activities have to go. Lian didn't have to give up her success, and unlike Joan Barnes, she didn't have to make any life-shattering changes, but she did need to make some difficult choices and reprioritize to bring the joy back into her work.

"I was in Kansas City with the Oprah tour; CBS had done a piece on us, filming us doing our work; we were in production six days a week; my hair looked great; but I was miserable," says Lian. She had to ask herself why she was trying to do everything at once.

While she was maxed out at work, she was still trying to volunteer at her sons' school. She remembers a day of hectic rescheduling, trying to solicit a donation for a balloon arch for a school event and make it to an important business meeting—it was all too much. She knew she had to take a break and realign her life.

The first thing she decided was to consciously start saying no. She clarified her basic priorities: first, kids; second, work; third, volunteer work. When a mother asked her if she would be the room parent the next school year, she said, "No! I don't want to be the room parent *ever*." She took a two-year hiatus from all volunteer work at the school. She said no to her son's soccer team and to unpaid speaking gigs—all good causes, but they took time away from higher-priority activities. She mastered a skill all working moms need to cultivate: learning to say no without hedging and without guilt.

## FIRST THINGS FIRST

To find true success, you have to assess your priorities at work and at home, and also make time to take care of yourself. Lian could fall back on organizational skills that she learned from her mother, a master organizer who ran an efficient household with eight kids. Her mom's motto: "First things first."

Lian brought the lessons she learned from her mom into her work life. She often told her production staff, first things first. The quality of the show and its guests was the number one priority. Anything else—marketing, expanding the Web site, doing keynotes—was always lower priority than keeping the quality of the show high. She reiterated this message to her staff over and over, knowing that it's easy for people to get lost in exciting new endeavors that don't link to the main goal. Now she runs her calendar the way the best leaders do: everything she dedicates her time to must be in service to her overriding goals, whether they are in support of her career, her family, or her health.

Lian brought her work skills home, too. She realized she had to make herself and her kids a higher priority. She put exercise back in her life and banned TV, a distraction from quality time with her children. She gets to bed early, wakes up before the kids so that she has quiet time to herself, and powers through a prioritized to-do list each day so that she can feel productive and enjoy her family in the evening. If she starts to feel impatient and quick to anger, she takes the time to clear the extraneous responsibilities from her calendar.

## TIME MANAGEMENT TOOLS

Working moms live in a perpetual state of imbalance; busy schedules and endless responsibilities are a given. I've grown accustomed to living on the outer edge of balance, especially since I added the role of author to my others: entrepreneur, wife, mom, daughter, board member, and friend. There are countless moments when my busy schedule threatens to tip me over so I have to stop and realign my priorities, such as when Leah shoved a hot-pink Post-it note under my office door one Saturday morning:

> Dear Mama,
>
> Me and Dada are for sure soul mates but I have given up on you. R.s.v.p. –Anonnamous

I gave myself a couple more guilt-free hours of writing that morning and then put my work aside to enjoy an afternoon with my daughters in the park.

We need to accept reality: living our multilayered lives comes at a cost. We can't do it all, or at least not all at once— much as we may try—but with the help of creative time management tools that help us bring good leadership into all of our life's domains, we can live full, satisfying lives that support our diverse interests.

## Life Wheel

You can see from Joan's and Lian's stories why assessing your priorities is important. Let's take a look at a tool that can help you track your time and shift your priorities if your calendar is sapping your energy.

When I coach women who are gearing up for a job change or returning to work after their baby is born, or who simply feel off kilter, I use a Life Wheel to determine which areas need more attention. Your "wheel" will inevitably roll along bumpily, but by identifying the roles and dimensions of your life that are important, you can achieve a smoother ride. Here's how it works:

**Relax.** You first need to find the time to relax physically and mentally in order to reflect and to filter out the chaos of daily life.

**Make a list** of seven to nine roles and dimensions in your life, such as work, home, community, and self. Here are examples from one of my client's wheels: spouse, mother, community, career, spirituality, self-care (bicycling, friends, and writing). Write them each down, one per spoke, on the lines of the template (p. 216).

**Figure out the time.** On a scale of 0 (low) to 5 (high), write down the amount of attention you currently give to each. Make a dot for each dimension and then connect the dots around the wheel to get a visual sense of which areas might deserve more or less focus. (See the sample wheel.)

Once you've completed your Life Wheel, take a moment to consider the following questions. Keep in mind that the goal is not to devote a high level of attention to every area. You know all too well the finite amount of time you have in a day.

On what activities do I want to spend *less* time? (Hint: think of those activities that give you little return on your investment of time and make you feel lethargic just to think about them.)

_____

_____

_____

Think about how to off-load undesired tasks. For example, to whom are you going to delegate? What are the obstacles to focusing less time here, and how will you get through this challenge?

_____

_____

_____

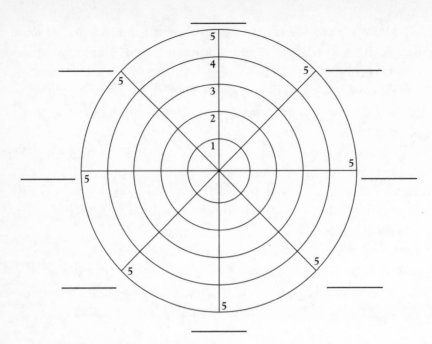

Life Wheel

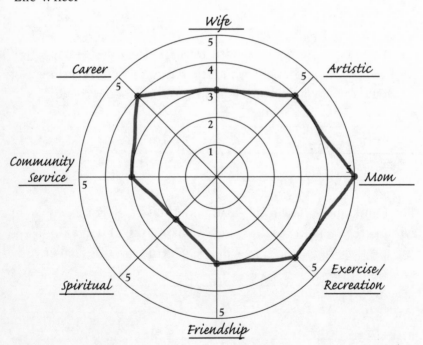

Life Wheel (Sample)

On what activities do I want to spend *more* time? (Hint: think about which activities you miss most when you leave them out.)

_____

_____

_____

What will you do to expand the time you devote to this area? What are the obstacles to focusing more time here, and how will you get through this challenge?

_____

_____

_____

□ □ □

Use this tool to open your mind to what's possible when you organize your time wisely. Instead of thinking about each aspect of your life as a competing separate entity, imagine your life with a better sense of harmony. Experiment with ways to cut what feels stagnant and try new ventures that respect your whole self.

## Tracking Your Time

How do you figure out which priorities come first? Daniel Gilbert, author of *Stumbling on Happiness*, advises people to "take ten seconds every hour and look at what you're doing from a higher place." A common pitfall is to spend time—whether at work or at home—on inconsequential tasks rather than making difficult choices and trade-offs. Another mistake people make is to think of different aspects of life as either-or propositions pitted against each other. What can you do to work more efficiently, focusing on your highest priorities, so that you bring the dimensions of your life into greater harmony?

By slowing down and tracking your time, you may find that you're spending too much of it on stupefying business meetings or too little of it exercising. Once you know your priorities and recognize the activities that are wasting your time and depleting your energy, the trick is to line up your time with what is most important and gives you satisfaction. It's a simple idea, yet most leaders and parents, when they track their time, are startled to discover that how they spend their time doesn't correspond to what they value most.

Another important idea is to creatively confront your time to figure out ways to fulfill two parts of yourself at once—for example, taking up skiing with your kids satisfies your family needs and, at the same time, takes care of your physical and recreational needs. You can have time with friends *and* your child by joining a mother-daughter book group. Sometimes you want better boundaries between work and home, but if you think about it, organizing your time better might mean looking at the different parts of your life more holistically.

You can manage your time better with the help of five questions:

1. What activities most engage you at home, at work, and personally?

| Home | Work | Yourself |
|------|------|----------|
|      |      |          |

2. Is the majority of your time spent on tasks linked to your highest, most engaging priorities? If not, what lower-value tasks that sap your passion can you minimize? What will you do to carve out time for your highest priorities?

3. What activities can you do that take care of two aspects of yourself at once—for example, can you do a spiritual activity with your family? do a community service activity with your colleagues? take a cooking class with your spouse, doing something you personally enjoy while also nurturing your marriage? merge a business trip with a family vacation?

4. Are you clear on the results you're trying to achieve with each task? What is the purpose, for example, of volunteering to be the president at your church? What need are you satisfying by serving on the wellness committee at work?

5. Technology is one of the biggest time traps. Do you put a limit on the time you spend checking e-mail or surfing the Web? Do you have times when you turn off your Blackberry, computer, and cell phone?

Before you begin each day, take some time to plot out how you're going to use your time. At the end of each day, clear your desk and make a well-organized to-do list for the next day so that you're ready to begin fresh in the morning. Think creatively, experimenting with small ways you can respect the various parts of yourself.

## PUT YOUR TIME WHERE YOUR HEART IS

How you spend your time at work shows your colleagues what you truly value. If you talk about the importance of collaboration and then make unilateral decisions, people will soon recognize that you don't really mean what you say. You can insist on great customer service, but if you spend no time yourself improving customer relations, you can't expect your employees to believe your words. Instead, they'll follow your example. Conversely, if you make the time for what you say is important, you not only send a message more powerful than words but also boost your credibility.

Regina Scott and Kate Jones, managers at a psychiatric hospital, demonstrated their values to their staff when they organized a team training to increase cohesion throughout the organization. When the question came up about how to get everyone trained together, including the night staff who worked from 11:00 PM to 7:00 AM, Regina and Kate jumped up to volunteer to work the night shift. The team cheered. The two managers generated goodwill by working through the night, living the values they espoused.

Suzanne Riss, editor-in-chief of *Working Mother* magazine, also leads by example. She feels passionate about helping working moms do great work and have a family life, so she makes it clear to her staff that they should go home to their families by six. She doesn't reward people for working late or for working long hours. She herself works from home every Monday so that she can take her son, Jack, to school, talk to his teachers, and pick him up at the end of the day. Every person who works for her has a flexible schedule, overlapping during six core hours between ten and four o'clock. Some telecommute.

"We believe what we write about in the magazine," Suzanne says. "You can work anytime, anywhere. You don't have to be chained to a desk to be productive. Giving flexibility to my staff builds loyalty and reduces stress."

The reality for many working mothers is that they can't get all their work done in eight hours, even if they're extremely efficient. This is the case in the magazine industry. Suzanne logs on to her computer early mornings, every weekend, and for a couple of hours after Jack goes to sleep. The difference is that whereas most other magazines keep staffs at the office working through dinner until 10 PM or later, people at *Working Mother* can go home to be with their families and then catch up on work after kids are asleep.

Suzanne realizes what many business leaders have shared with me—that working mothers are often the most industrious workers because they don't have the luxury to socialize at the watercooler or take long lunches. They want to get their work done as efficiently as possible so that they can spend time with their families.

## SHIFTING TO KID TIME

The efficiency ethic that works in the office doesn't work at home. Kid time requires that you slow down and go with the flow. Any attempts I make to hurry my children inevitably backfire. The more I dash, the more they dawdle. I've learned to let go of my impatience when my younger daughter takes forever to walk a city block, appreciating that she notices things that I would otherwise miss—a ladybug on the sidewalk or an Astroturf-covered car.

If you try to impose your office efficiency tactics on your kids, you'll be disappointed. Suzanne Riss realized that the kind of structured organization that makes her and her staff so efficient at work doesn't always translate when it comes to her role as a mother. She remembers when Jack was sick, and she arranged an hour out of her work schedule to meet the babysitter and Jack at the doctor's office. The doctor was running late, which she hadn't factored into her schedule. And then when it came time for her to go back to work, Jack called out, "Mommy, don't leave me." Listening to Jack's wails as the babysitter's car sped away, Suzanne wondered, *Why am I rushing back to work?* She recalls, "My son needed me that day more than work did. That day I learned a lesson: priorities can change in a moment. I needed to be more fluid. We have choices every day."

It's often hard to mentally shift to kid time after putting in a long day at work. Many mothers find that they need to build in transition time to make the shift from worker to mom. Brain researchers at Carnegie Mellon University acknowledge that it takes purposeful effort and a period of time for the mind to adjust to a different task; it's as if we are loading a different program on our computer.

Some working mothers use commute time to write their to-do lists, ruminate on work concerns, and then clear their minds so that they can give their children their full attention. Writer and mother Lee Hsu wrote through the day until one hour before her sons came home from school. Knowing she wasn't able to shift to motherhood easily after a day of writing, she spent an hour gardening, clearing her mind to prepare for switching roles.

"When I didn't take this hour to mentally shift, I found myself wanting the kids to disappear so I could continue to write. By taking this hour, I was better able to be there and to remember that my time with my kids was very limited and they grow up so fast," says Lee. Now that her kids are grown, she sums it up this way: "You need to do something you love, that brings you joy, something that doesn't involve being a mom. And then when you're with your kids, you need to keep work at bay. That's how I was able to feel like a whole person."

## FINDING THE RIGHT JOB

Literally every working mother I spoke with said that when she is truly engaged at work, it's good for her family. When you're excited about meaningful work, you're happy at work *and* at home. When the job starts to feel like a slog and drains your energy, perhaps it's time to make a change. For example, Molly Rosen was a vice president of a large training company when she quit her job. She was turning forty, her confidence was high, but she was burning out. She worked fifty hours each week, traveling every other week, and had missed important events in her children's lives, including a bout with pneumonia and her son's first steps.

She and her husband knew that their pace was taking its toll on the family. Molly knew she had to find a more satisfying professional endeavor. She left her job and took on an exciting project editing and launching an anthology about women in their forties.

"Part of my job was coaching executives. I saw many of them not giving their best at their job because they lacked the passion. They were burned out just like me. I felt inauthentic coaching them, feeling that I, too, wasn't giving my best at work or at home," said Molly. She knew she wanted to work outside the home because she loved to be part of a cause, and working gave her a feeling of achievement.

"I feel like I am a better mom when I satisfy my need for achievement and professional development. I get those needs met at work," said Molly. But she had reached her limit and had to find a job that offered her more flexibility and new challenges. It took courage and a good amount of soul searching for Molly to walk away from good money and a secure job to do what was right for her family.

How can you make a living doing what suits your interests and skills? The best leaders find careers that tap into their individual needs, skills, and interests. You might hear a voice in your head that says, "I can't make a living doing what I love." It's true—no one loves all aspects of her job, but if you can't find any positives in your work, or if you used to like parts of your job but now feel stagnant, it's time to abandon resignation and ask some hard questions.

Edgar H. Schein at MIT has identified eight "career anchors" and has shown that people find greater job satisfaction when their work matches their preferred competencies. For example, a person with a preference for security-stability will seek stable employment, staying away from jobs that require her to take risks. Look at the eight career anchors and identify which ones reflect you best.

1. Technical-functional competence. People with this preference like to gain mastery and deep expertise. They like to apply their skills to understanding how things work and to solving problems.

2. General managerial competence. These people enjoy interacting with other people on a regular basis. They like to support people's learning, build teams, and provide mentoring. To be effective in this area, they also need emotional intelligence.

3. Autonomy-independence. These people thrive when they are able to work independently with their own standards and rules.

4. Security-stability. Security-focused people seek stability and continuity as primary factors in their lives. They avoid risks and tend to stay in one job for a long period of time.

5. Entrepreneurial creativity. Entrepreneurial people thrive on creativity and autonomy. They easily get bored and prefer to invent things and take ownership.

6. Service and dedication to a cause. Service-oriented people are driven by how they can help other people, and tend to work in public service or nonprofits.

7. Pure challenge. People driven by challenge seek constant stimulation and difficult problems that they can tackle. Such people need jobs that offer continual variation and a broad spectrum of challenges.

8. Lifestyle. Lifestyle-driven people are more interested in indulging their passion for travel or other interests and would likely be unhappy in a routine office job. They tend to see work and life as one integrated whole.

Is your job in sync with your preferences? If not, maybe it's time for a change. Find people who have jobs that sound interesting to you and who seem happy with their work. Ask them for an informational interview. Do your research. Your career is too big a part of your life for you to give up on the possibility of a better fit between you and your job.

## INDULGE YOURSELF

The balance of work and home also has to include nurturing yourself. For too many of us, self-care is the first thing to go. To spend your precious time wisely and not get worn down by the relentless demands of work and motherhood, you need to know when exhaustion is setting in and find the time to rejuvenate.

Alice Fishman, a former business manager, goes away with women friends at least three times each year, no matter how busy her life. She feels little guilt because she knows that when she hits her limit, she's not much use to her family—in fact, with her patience paper-thin, she feels she's doing everyone a favor when she makes her escape. To get away is no easy task— she organizes elaborate calendars, choreographs play dates, and extracts favors from others to drive her kids to their various activities. But it's well worth the effort. Last year, she and a friend went to New York City for a week.

"I felt parts of myself I don't normally pay attention to at home and at work. When I returned I was much more present and patient with my kids, and I appreciated them and the life that I have more. It lingers for a few days, and then I need to find small ways to refuel again," says Alice.

Many moms have to get through a certain amount of guilt before they can take what they feel is a self-indulgent step for themselves. Film critic Beverly Berning was feeling tired constantly, unable to give much to her daughters. She had long dreamed of a trip to Paris, where she had lived for five years when in her twenties. She bought a ticket for her fiftieth birthday, but as the date approached, she decided that maybe she shouldn't go, especially given that her relationship with her twelve-year-old daughter had become tumultuous.

"I thought maybe I shouldn't go. My kids need me. My relationship with my daughter was strained. But then I thought maybe I need to go *because* my kids need me," said Beverly. She went to Paris for ten days by herself. Spending time wandering the streets of Paris, not as a mom or a wife, she felt a wholeness and happiness that was stifled by the day-in, day-out demands of her role as a writer, a mother, and a wife. She came back revived and ready to give more to her family.

Every mom I spoke with who described revitalizing escapes from family life came back feeling equipped to be a better mom. In my role as a leadership coach, one of the first lessons I teach everyone—from executives to religious leaders—is this: to perform your best and inspire the best in others, you need to step back from the pressure and nurture yourself. I've found it's easier to convince dads to do this than moms, who often feel guilty that they aren't giving enough of themselves to their kids. But once I finally do talk women into taking a mini break, their "I need time for me" impulses, long buried deep in their mommy brains, wake up. Whether they're running a company or a carpool, when they don't take a breather, their joy is too often displaced by feelings of stress, resentment, and pointless drudgery. In fact, a recent BizRate survey reflects the burden that many mothers experience: out of 1,062 moms polled, almost half (47 percent) said they were the "least happy person in the household." Yikes.

So how do I persuade busy, ambitious moms to take a time out? By using this introspective quiz that I designed with Carol Evans of Working Mother Media. I issue a challenge to you: What would you do if you could take three hours all to yourself? Before you unleash excuses as to why you couldn't possibly do this, humor me. The quiz takes just a few minutes, so start thinking about what you'd do.

Here are some ground rules for this daydream: you can't spend the hours with your spouse or your kids. They must be spent indulgently, selfishly. Given three extra hours, some moms instantly say, "I'll spend them with my kids." The point of this exercise is to help you come to a connect-the-dots moment in which you realize the delight and joy in your life and reawaken the passion you feel for your work, life, and family. Chances are, you are not going to get there while playing another round of Candy Land.

A big benefit for moms who nurture themselves is that spouses and kids report feeling happier with their rejuvenated partners and moms. Realizing that mom is happier when she's rested, family members often push mom out the door for regular mommy retreats.

Here we go:

1. You pull double shifts taking care of everyone else, yet your neglect yourself. What drives you to do this? Guilt that you're not spending enough time with your kids? Concern that you're falling behind in your career? List three reasons why you feel you can't slow down.

_____

_____

_____

Now imagine that you have to slow down. What would happen?

_____

_____

_____

2. Write down a guilty-mom moment that still makes you cringe.

_____

_____

_____

Now think about whether there were unexpected benefits to your cringe moment that you can see in retrospect. For example, suppose that your son said, "All my friends' mommies pick them up right after school. Why do I have to go to after-care?" You can ask, Did he actually enjoy after-care? Did he make new friends? Try to find something redemptive that came from that moment.

_____

_____

_____

3. What makes you feel guilty on a regular basis? Is it Evan's mom doing museum-worthy art projects with her kids while yours make do with a bucket of crayons? Is it leaving your sick child with a babysitter instead of being with her yourself?

_____

_____

_____

4. List the three activities you most dislike doing with your kids. Dread supervising math homework? Resent driving them to karate on Saturday mornings?

_____

_____

_____

Choose one activity that you could stop doing today. (Introduce your spouse to the joys of karate carpool.)

_____

_____

_____

Choose another activity you could get help with. (Could you recruit a high school student as a tutor?)

_____

_____

_____

5. List three things you realistically could do to make your life easier at home.

_____

_____

_____

What stops you from doing each of these things?

_____

_____

_____

Now take a hard look at your excuses. No money for help with the housework? Is there something you could cut from your budget to afford help once a month? Choose one of your lamest excuses and find a solution.

_____

_____

_____

6. Imagine that all your responsibilities are on hold for three hours. What would you do with that free time all to yourself? How would it make you a better mom, partner, employee, person?

_____

_____

_____

7. Name someone you'd call in a crisis or someone who could help you get back on track if you drift off course.

_____

_____

_____

8. Guess what? You just figured out where you can get three guilt-free hours to nurture yourself (see your answers to questions 4 and 5). You've also figured out why you so desperately need this time (see your answer to question 6). Now commit to it. You officially have permission to take three hours off, so get out your calendar and block out the time. To keep you committed, have the person from question 7 sign the bottom of this page. This person is going to hold you to it. Now go. Be guilt-free!

## BALANCING TOGETHER

Balancing work and home is a two-person job: it requires both parents to work together to support their child, while at the same time balancing work commitments outside the home and personal commitments to their own nonparent needs—no easy task! Sharing domestic chores requires good communication, and even then, things break down. For one thing, let's face it: all the good intentions in the world don't lead to a clean solution. In my house, even if we truly share the load 50-50, even if the kids do their chores, I doubt that we'll lie around relaxed all the time wondering what all the fuss about work-life balance is about. Sharing the load in my house simply means that we're both exhausted by the end of the day.

Another reason we face a losing battle with the work-life balance thing is that we're running up against outmoded cultural messages that are hard to change. I'm struck by how often even the most egalitarian-minded parents can fall into a mindset that the woman is in charge when it comes to household duties and child care, even when both parents work outside the home. My mom, a working mother and ardent feminist, often remarked how wonderful it was to see my husband change diapers, as if he were doing me some sort of favor to take care of his own child. Mothers of my own generation fall into outdated thinking too. Pediatrician Rona Bar Din told me she always reminded her three daughters to thank Daddy for dinner when they went out to restaurants, mimicking her own mother, who expected Rona and her sisters to thank their father for dinner each night. Only years later did she realize how insidious the cultural norms are and how easy it was, even for dual-income families, to fall into old-fashioned thinking about gender roles.

## Scale Back at Work

How do you work on creating satisfying roles at home? For some parents, cultivating more equally shared parenting means scaling back the time spent at work—not always possible given the typically inflexible nine-to-five work structure in the United States. Marc and Amy Vachon challenged the conventional full-time work mold and imbalanced divisions of child-care responsibilities: they launched a Web site called equallysharedparenting.com to help parents infuse more equality into parenting. Marc, an information technologist, and Amy, a pharmacist, both work part-time so that they can more easily divide housework and parenting duties. With two children, Maia, six, and Theo, three, they manage to enjoy their jobs, their hobbies, their children, and each other. But it isn't easy. Marc is the only man at his company to take a reduced workweek (and reduced paycheck), and Amy struggles to stick to her convictions when every mom in her mom's group elected to give up their careers to stay home with their children. When Marc asked his boss for a reduced workweek, his boss was worried that everyone would want to follow suit. Not one man opted for reducing his work schedule, all unwilling to take the smaller paycheck.

"I listened to all these moms who opted to stay home talk about their husbands as hopeless, gone all the time to pursue their high-powered jobs. I was the only mom in the group who couldn't meet in the middle of the day. There wasn't room for my point of view. They couldn't fathom that my husband wasn't super powered and that I wanted to go back to work; I moved on to a working mom group, where the idea for Equally Shared Parenting germinated," says Amy.

Both Amy and Marc acknowledge that it takes guts to share parenting equally.

"There are sacrifices you have to make, financial trade-offs. We want to work, get paid accordingly, and live a life pursuing something we enjoy. Amy plays her violin and I bicycle and play tennis. We live a relatively simple life but it has taken a conscious effort to make choices that support a balanced lifestyle," says Marc.

Marc and Amy recognize that the hardest part, aside from a reduced income, is to comanage without the woman directing her husband's every move.

"Women have to work on their sales pitch, or else the husband says, 'Why would I want to do more work around the house?' The idea is that the shared lifestyle benefits both, as well as the kids," says Marc. But it's easier said than done.

It takes two important steps to achieve more equal parenting. First, recognize the cultural messages and question traditional assumptions about parenting roles and expectations. Second, decide what cultural norms you want to reject—for example, do you want to opt out of the nine-to-five full-time work schedule or climbing the corporate ladder? Marc and Amy confronted the work-life models that ate away at their recreation and family time, and advocated for a part-time work schedule that gave them a more balanced life. This won't work for every family, but the important thing is to question the pervasive cultural expectations that can squelch your happiness.

## Make an Agreement

You can help your marriage by consciously agreeing on your priorities and collaborating. Trudi and Andrew Roth took the leap to confront their unbalanced lives and drew up a marriage agreement. The two of them had to endure a stressful year when Trudi's job wasn't fulfilling and their marriage was stressed for Trudi to realize that she was fed up with shouldering more than her fair share of the domestic workload. So, inspired by *The Mommy Myth*, by Susan Douglas and Meredith Michaels, Trudi and Andrew drew up an agreement, complete with eighty-nine tasks that had to get done each week to manage their family, including dressing the kids, emptying the dishwasher, paying bills, getting the kids out the door for school, going to dental appointments, getting haircuts, registering for Sunday school, hiring babysitters, and feeding pets. *Eighty-nine tasks.* No wonder we're stressed.

# Marriage Agreement

### Trudi Smith Roth & Andrew Roth

In recognition of the fact that we, Trudi and Andy, both opted to have children and become a family, the following marriage agreement has been created to acknowledge and divide the responsibilities and work that goes into creating a home and hearth for all members of our family. While assumptions based on gender surround us on a daily basis—in the media, in our families, friends and neighbors—we realize that we have the power to fairly share the load, regardless of our sex, our financial contributions or our competence in a given area.

Furthermore, each member of the family has an equal right to her/his own time, work, values and choices. Domestic jobs must be considered and divided, as agreed upon by the partners in the marriage. If one party works overtime in any domestic job, she/he must be compensated by equal work by the other. Communication is essential—if both parties agree to modify terms of this agreement, then it shall be. Without communication, there is no modification of the division of labor.

Finally, this agreement is drafted in the spirit of partnership, of shared responsibility and of commitment to each other and to our children.

## Share the Load with Your Children

Somehow my husband and I fell down as leaders: our kids missed the lesson about pitching in. As much as we talk about the importance of sharing the load, our lovely daughters are uninspired when it comes to chores. I don't want my kids to wait until they become parents to understand and appreciate just how much Mommy and Daddy do for them. But no matter how much we talked about the chore inequities in our house, we weren't getting through—until I tried Heather's tactic.

Heather Swallow, an accountant and a mother of three daughters under thirteen, used this strategy for fostering appreciation of what it takes to run a household. She came up with her approach after she was worn out trying to juggle work, her daughter's ballet schedule, and her other daughter's competitive soccer schedule:

1. Ask your children to write down on a piece of paper all the things they can think of that Mommy and Daddy do to support them and the household. When they are done, ask them to write a list of all the things they themselves need to do during the day and the things they do to support the household.

2. Then begin the conversation. This is *not* about a guilt trip. You simply start the conversation by saying, "What do you think about these lists?" You probably won't need to say much more to get a creative conversation going. From there, you have a great starting place for generating new behavior.

In Heather's case, her children wrote up a list of ways they would help more around the house. They drew chore charts and hung them on the kitchen wall. At last report, the children were doing far more chores than Heather ever dreamed possible.

I did this with my kids at one of our Sunday evening family meetings, and it worked well. With some occasional booster shots, the strategy helps our house run more efficiently and helps me and my husband stay ahead of absolute chaos.

## DESPERATELY SEEKING FLEXIBILITY

Among the women in the mom's support group I joined when Anna was born, figuring out how to balance the dueling demands of career and motherhood was the number one issue. We had no inkling that a child would take up our life in such a joyful but consuming way. When one mom warned us, after watching an *Oprah* episode, that nannies neglect children when mommies go off to work, we went ballistic—being hormonal and sleep deprived didn't help. Even though I knew rationally that the *Oprah* horror stories were exaggerated to instill fear and guilt in working mothers, I already could see that I needed to find a way out of my full-time pressure-filled job. I negotiated a 60 percent–time workweek, splitting my duties with another mother. My group's dilemma inspired me to launch a consulting company called The Balancing Act, now called The Parent Leader, and I coached women on how to create nontraditional work plans. Even with flexible work arrangements, the path has its downsides, including slower promotions, smaller paychecks, decreased credibility, and resentment on the part of colleagues and bosses. Working mothers need to be savvy about how to set up flexible work schedules that are mutually beneficial to them and their employers.

A growing number of workplaces have figured out that work schedule flexibility is a win-win cost-saving business strategy. Even parents lucky enough to work for organizations with flexible work arrangements are likely to think twice before broaching the topic with their bosses. Sure, your boss may say it's fine to go ahead and work part-time, but realize there are trade-offs. A part-time schedule may slow your climb up the organizational ladder, and you'll need to make sure you can make ends meet with a smaller paycheck.

Before knocking on your boss's door to ask for a compressed workweek or Fridays off, consider the following strategies to increase the likelihood that redesigning your schedule is a win for you and your employer:

1. **Figure out what you really want.** Is it to work thirty hours? to be home each day by 3:00? What financial compromises can you make? Evaluate what would make the biggest difference in easing your stress and giving you the time you need.

2. **Learn from others.** Talk to other parents with flexible work arrangements. What can you learn from their experiences?

3. **Anticipate obstacles.** Think through how you'll cover vacations, overtime, and crunch times. Work out the details about how clients can contact you, even on the days you work at home. How will you cause the least disruption to your coworkers?

4. **Assess your value.** Your case will be more convincing if you take stock of what you contribute, including your years of service, unique skill set, and knowledge of the institution.

5. **Think six months out.** Plan to reevaluate the arrangement in three to six months so that your boss doesn't feel locked in.

6. **Put your request in writing.** Your proposal should include the following parts:
   a. Specific details about the kind of work schedule you want and when you'd like to begin.

b.  How you plan to deal with crunch times, meetings on your off days, travel, and client needs and perceptions.

c.  How you plan to stay in touch with the office when you're not physically on site.

d.  Benefits to your employer—for example, retaining an experienced employee and avoiding recruitment and retraining costs, reducing benefit costs, and enhancing the company's reputation as a family-friendly employer. Remember that your boss wants to know how the work will get done, not how flextime will allow you to attend soccer games. Diplomatically point out that study after study shows that flexible work schedules positively influence productivity, absenteeism, and morale.

e.  Specify which, if any, job duties you need to reassign.

Even when you plan well, your boss is likely to raise objections. Here are several typical reservations with suggested responses. Make a list of other objections you're likely to hear and prepare a well-thought-out response:

**Boss:** I'm concerned that if I say yes to you, everyone else is going to want a flexible schedule.
**You:** Although others may like the idea, I believe that most people can't afford the cut in pay or benefits.

□ □ □

**Boss:** I'm fine with your proposal, but I don't think your clients or staff will be happy with this arrangement.
**You:** I will continue to check my e-mail and voice mail from home and respond to client requests within twenty-four hours, just as I have always done. I don't think my clients will notice my change in schedule, and I don't think they need to know that there is any change. As for my employees, this will be no different than when I'm out on travel or at

meetings. They will have access to me via e-mail and phone just as they do now.

Boss: I haven't seen this work well in the past. I'm inclined to say no.

You: Are you willing to try this arrangement for three months and then reevaluate?

Once you've made a new option work for you, you may run into a few snags along the way. For example:

**You find yourself working the same number of hours, but now you're getting paid less.** Set limits and stick to them, or reevaluate your agreement so that you get paid for hours worked.

**You get passed over for exciting projects or promotions.** Communicate about desired assignments in the same direct way as you did to renegotiate your work schedule. Stay visible and express interest in assuming increased responsibility, even if your workweek is reduced.

**You miss meetings in which important information is shared.** Greet flexibility with flexibility. Be strategic about which meetings you're willing to come in for, even when you're not scheduled to be at work. Ask others to share meeting notes or put you on speaker phone.

**Your coworkers resent you.** Or maybe you feel guilty when you leave at 3:00, so you imagine antagonism. Either way, ask, "Is there anything you'd like me to do differently so that my new schedule creates the least disruption for the project we're working on together?" Work together to offset challenges and generate collaborative solutions. Check in with coworkers periodically to keep communication open.

## A WORD ABOUT SOCIETAL ROADBLOCKS

Even the most successful leaders and parents face times when their lives feel severely out of balance. And it's no wonder. We've set an unachievable standard of ardent careerism coupled with an obsession with our children. Wouldn't it be nice to get a windfall of assistance from the government or business world to ease the pressure? Universal health care, subsidized day care, flexible work schedules, and quality public education would be an excellent start to relieve the stresses and strains of working and parenting. I hope we all open our eyes to societal problems and speak up for needed change. I don't want to let sluggish workplace reform stop me from cultivating the life I want, but at the same time, I want to do what I can to influence change at the local and federal levels. Here are a couple of things you can do:

Visit www.workingmother.com to find out about the 100 Best Companies for mothers, conferences, Web seminars, leadership summits, and breakfast meetings to address a wide spectrum of issues affecting working mothers.

Become involved in making positive change for families in this country by joining MomsRising.org, a grassroots, nonpartisan, Web-based organization. Joining is free, and the organization notifies members of national and state campaigns and makes it easy to write letters and sign petitions for such issues as paid family leave, fair pay for mothers, keeping toys safe, or stopping cuts to child-care and after-school-care programs.

## WORKING IS GOOD FOR YOUR CHILDREN

There's no way to avoid getting pulled in two (or three or ten) directions when you're a working mother. It's unavoidable that you will have to bring work home sometimes. And there will be important events you'll miss in your child's life. But think about this: moms who work are setting a positive example for their children. If your child sees you pursuing your professional goals or experiencing joy in activities outside the home, she is freed up to foster her individuality. Daughters learn a model which demonstrates that you can be an involved mom and a worker—you can have it all (you just need to put up with a certain amount of stress and chaos)—and sons develop respect for women's capability in the work world and for women's independence.

According to the U.S. Bureau of Labor Statistics, twenty-six million mothers work, contributing $476 billion to U.S. household incomes. Are millions of mothers harming their children by going to work? We've struggled with the stigma that working mothers neglect their children to some degree. But there is little evidence that moms who work harm their children. In fact, a report released by the Families and Work Institute showed that children of working mothers have higher math and reading achievement levels and higher self-esteem, and they are more self-reliant at home. "Kids learn positive lessons by watching their mothers operate in the outside world, taking action, exerting influence, making decisions, and using their talents," says Ellen Galinsky, president and cofounder of the Families and Work Institute.

I know I learned important lessons about the value of work by watching my mom work throughout my growing up. I watched my mom grade papers at night while I did my homework, and I remember feeling proud that my mom was a teacher. I learned the importance of financial independence, especially given that my mom raised me single-handedly. Although I didn't like it when she hired a babysitter when I was sick so that she could go to work, I learned the value of holding to a commitment. As my friends know, I can get on a soapbox about the virtues of women working, but the bottom line is having work that gives you a paycheck and a creative outlet, and allows you to feel connected to something meaningful and bigger than just yourself.

□□□

Most of us buzz through our day barely stopping to breathe. Then we find ourselves wrung out by the end of the day, unable to enjoy our families. But what about those times when you do work you love *and* enjoy kid time *and* take care of yourself? It takes a conscious effort and some courage and creativity to figure out how to juggle everything. It means making tough choices and consciously building time for what you value—not what you think you *should* value. To weave our many roles into our busy lives and still stay refreshed by the end of the day requires a sharp focus on what really matters.

We also need realistic expectations. Tension between the various roles and responsibilities in our lives is inevitable, and the fantasy that as working mothers we can live in perfect balance is just one more thing to make us feel inadequate—but we can live a more fulfilling, authentic life when we act with integrity and use our time wisely.

In the Conclusion, we'll look at how you can use each of the seven leadership strategies explored in this book to fully embrace your role as Mom-in-Chief. You'll see how bringing the best leadership practices home, especially when you're faced with dilemmas and no easy answers, is sure to yield better results.

# Conclusion
## Bringing It All Home

It's true: the strategies you use at work can work at home. We've seen many examples of how the basic tenets of good leadership work as well at the kitchen table as in the board room. The result is not only a more successful family life but also a deeper connection with your kids and partner.

There's no question that being a Mom-in-Chief can be more difficult when emotions run high. Keeping leadership strategies in mind when you are faced with a stormy situation at home isn't always easy. But if you pause and use the tools in this book, you're apt to have fewer tears and a lot more success.

I recently faced a tough dilemma that gave me the chance to try out these techniques at home. I got a call that Anna's week-long backpacking trip was cancelled due to low enrollment, but the camp director was happy to roll her and her friends over to a whitewater rafting trip instead.

My first thought: *Don't people die on rafting trips in rough rivers?* I could picture it in my mind: Anna is bouncing around on a roiling, whitewater river; they take a wrong turn; the boat wraps around a rock; her head submerges, hits a rock; she never floats back to surface. No way was she going rafting.

Burke had another point of view. My cautious husband read the brochure, said it was an easy river to raft, and thought it would be fun. Anna was ambivalent—she has no experience with moving water—but wanted to go off on an adventure with her friends. Normally, as long as my kids are with their father, whom I know to be safety conscious, I'm able to put my fears aside and feel good about their various rock-climbing, cave-exploring, and high-diving adventures. I know better than to spoil their excitement and undermine their confidence with my fears. But I couldn't get that image of my daughter hurtling toward a rock out of my head.

What's a leader to do? I took a deep breath and tried to draw on the seven strategies covered in this book.

### Strategy One: Setting Big-Picture Goals

What's the long view? My husband and I agreed that our goals were to build Anna's confidence and decision-making skills. If I let my fears drive the decision, would I obstruct our big-picture goal, taking away Anna's chance to build confidence? But couldn't she build confidence by doing something safe? What about public speaking?

### Strategy Two: Discovering Your Mom Mode

My Mom Mode—Connector—was running amok as I tried to stifle my fantasies of the worst-case fatal scenario. I tried to think of alternatives, such as baking pies or watching her favorite movies all week or playing tennis. But as a Connector, I had to acknowledge my daughter's needs and desires. So it was back to the big picture: building confidence.

### Strategy Three: Managing Conflict

I was spoiling for a fight. I needed to express my fears about the rafting trip, but also to listen to Burke when he told me that it was on only a Class III river and would not be a death-defying ride.

### Strategy 4: Creating Culture

Our family culture encourages our children to make their own good decisions. So we decided—in keeping with our big picture—to have Anna herself get some information about the rafting trip, finding out how dangerous it might be. Meanwhile, I called my friend Jane, who used to be a river rafting guide. Jane said, "She's more likely to die in a car crash on the way there than die on that particular river."

### Strategy 5: Managing Crisis

In the midst of my fears about the rafting trip, I felt as though we were facing a minor crisis. When I stepped back, however, I realized it was really just a challenging situation that we could all learn from. Not that I'm going rafting myself anytime soon.

### Strategy 6: Navigating the Growing Pains of Adolescence

I wanted to know whether Anna was being influenced by peer pressure. Was she ignoring the risks because her friends were pressuring her to go? We sounded her out about that, and were reassured that she'd gathered the information she needed and wasn't basing her decision on what her friends were saying.

### Strategy 7: Balancing Priorities

When my father-in-law wanted to climb to the top of Half Dome in Yosemite with Anna, Leah, and her cousins, I said no; I felt intense relief and never second-guessed my decision.

There's a line over which I can't go. But once we had more information about this rafting trip, I realized that even though I wasn't enthusiastic, the risks were small, and I could honor my daughter's decision to go.

□□□

What an experience!

You too can use the strategies in this book to enhance your growth and development as a leader. This means translating insight into action: discarding old habits that take you away from your big-picture goals and acting in a way that deepens your connection with your child, builds her confidence, and unleashes her full potential—and yours. Being a parent leader isn't easy; it takes practice, and you'll likely make more than a few mistakes along the way. Forgiving yourself, learning from your mistakes, and moving on are all essential elements to being a great parent.

My hope is that by placing parenting in the context of transformational leadership, you rise above overprotectiveness, anger, using your kids' achievements to reflect well on you—and begin to make decisions from a long-range perspective.

Here's one very important last point. To have the best connection with our children and the most positive influence on them, we need to deepen our connection with ourselves. We need courage and self-awareness in order to make full use of the best strategies that good leadership wisdom has to offer. We also need patience and realistic expectations. Don't expect to master the art of parenting overnight—it's a lifelong learning process, but one of the most rewarding ones life has to offer. Good luck to you and your family!

# REFERENCES

## Introduction

Burns, James MacGregor. *Leadership*. New York: HarperCollins, 1979.

## Leadership Strategy 1

Dweck, Carol. *Mindset: The New Psychology of Success*. New York: Ballantine, 2008.

## Leadership Strategy 2

Ehrensaft, Diane. *Parenting Together*. Champaign: University of Illinois Press, 1990.

Hersey, Paul, and Ron Campbell. *Situational Parenting*. Escondido, Calif.: Center for Leadership Studies, 1999.

## Leadership Strategy 4

Dweck, Carol. *Mindset: The New Psychology of Success*. New York: Ballantine Books, 2008.

McMahon, Regan. *Revolution in the Bleachers: How Parents Can Take Back Family Life in a World Gone Crazy over Youth Sports*. New York: Gotham Books, 2007.

Yokoyama, John, and Joseph Michelli. *When Fish Fly: Lessons for Creating a Vital and Energized Workplace.* New York: Hyperion, 2004.

## Leadership Strategy 5

Benard, Bonnie. *Resiliency: What We Have Learned.* San Francisco: WestEd, 2004.

Brooks, Robert, and Sam Goldstein. *Fostering Resilience in Our Children.* New York: McGraw-Hill, 2002.

Goleman, Daniel. *Emotional Intelligence: Why It Can Matter More Than IQ.* New York: Bantam Books, 1995.

Goleman, Daniel. "What Makes a Leader?" *Harvard Business Review,* Jan. 1998, pp. 82–91.

Goleman, Daniel. *Working with Emotional Intelligence.* New York: Bantam Books, 1998.

Goleman, Daniel. "Leadership That Gets Results." *Harvard Business Review,* Apr. 2000, pp. 78–90.

Goleman, Daniel, Robert Boyatzis, and Annie McKee. *Primal Leadership: Realizing the Power of Emotional Intelligence.* Boston: Harvard Business School Press, 2002.

Maddi, Salvatore R. "Hardiness Training at Illinois Bell Telephone." In Joseph P. Opatz (Ed.), *Health Promotion Evaluation.* Stevens Point, Wis.: National Wellness Institute, 1987.

Maddi, Salvatore R., and Suzanne C. Kobasa. *The Hardy Executive: Health Under Stress.* Homewood. Ill.: Dow Jones-Irwin, 1984.

Segal, Julius, and Zelda Segal. *Growing Up Smart and Happy.* New York: McGraw-Hill, 1985.

## Leadership Strategy 6

Blum, Robert William. *Mothers' Influence on Teen Sex: Connections That Promote Postponing Sexual Intercourse.* Presented at the Center for Adolescent Health and Development, University of Minnesota, Minneapolis, 2002.

Blum, Robert William, Clea McNeely, and Peggy Mann Rinehart. *Improving the Odds: The Untapped Power of Schools to Improve the Health of Teens.* Center for Adolescent Health and Development,

University of Minnesota, 2002. Available at www.sfu.ca/cfrj/fulltext/blum.pdf.

Csikszentmihalyi, Mihaly, Kevin Xathunde, and Samuel Whalen. *Talented Teenagers*. New York: Cambridge University Press, 1993.

QEV Analytics. *The Importance of Family Dinners*. National Center on Addiction and Substance Abuse at Columbia University, 2003. Available at www.casacolumbia.org.

Riera, Michael. *Staying Connected to Your Teenager: How to Keep Them Talking to You and How to Hear What They're Really Saying*. Cambridge, Mass.: Perseus, 2003.

Riera, Michael, and Joseph Di Prisco. *Right from Wrong: Instilling a Sense of Integrity in Your Child*. Cambridge, Mass.: Perseus, 2002, 2005.

Thomas-Lepore, Caitlin, Jennifer Bohanek, Robyn Fivush, and Marshall Duke. *"Today I ..."*: *Ritual and Spontaneous Narratives During Family Dinners*. Emory Center for Myth and Ritual in American Life, Working Paper No. 31, Apr. 2004.

Van Petten, Vanessa. *You're Grounded!* Bloomington, Ind.: iUniverse, 2007.

Whitlock, Janis. *Places to Be and Places to Belong: Youth Connectedness in School and Community*. ACT for Youth Upstate Center of Excellence, Cornell University, 2004.

## Leadership Strategy 7

Blades, Joan, and Kristin Rowe-Finkbeiner. *The Motherhood Manifesto: What America's Moms Want—and What to Do About It*. New York: Nation Books, 2006.

Evans, Carol. *This Is How We Do It: The Working Mothers' Manifesto*. New York: Hudson Street Press, 2006.

Gilbert, Daniel. *Stumbling on Happiness*. New York: Knopf, 2006.

Schein, Edgar H. *Career Anchors: Self Assessment*. Hoboken, N.J.: Wiley, 2006.

# RECOMMENDED READING

Ashworth, Trisha, and Amy Nobile. *I Was a Really Good Mom Before I Had Kids: Reinventing Modern Motherhood*. San Francisco: Chronicle Books, 2007.

Bennis, Warren. "The Leadership Advantage." *Leader to Leader*, Spring 1999, *12*, 18–23.

Bianchi, Suzanne, John P. Robinson, and Melissa A. Milkie. *Changing Rhythms of American Family Life*. New York: Russell Sage Foundation, 2007.

Blum, Robert William. "A Case for School Connectedness." *Adolescent Learner*, 2005, *62*(7), 16–20.

Blum, Robert William, Clea McNeely, and James Nonnemaker. "Vulnerability, Risk, and Protection." *Journal of Adolescent Health*, July 2002, *31*(1 Suppl.), 28–39.

Brooks, Robert, and Sam Goldstein. *The Power of Resilience*. New York: McGraw-Hill, 2004.

Crittenden, Ann. *The Price of Motherhood: Why the Most Important Job in the World Is Still the Least Valued*. New York: Henry Holt, 2001.

Csikszentmihalyi, Mihaly. *Good Business: Leadership, Flow, and the Making of Meaning*. New York: Penguin Books, 2003.

Deal, Terrence E., and Allan A. Kennedy. *Corporate Culture: The Rites and Rituals of Corporate Life*. Cambridge, Mass.: Perseus, 1982, 2000.

Di Prisco, Joseph, and Michael Riera. *Field Guide to the American Teenager: A Parent's Companion*. Cambridge, Mass.: Perseus, 2001.

Douglas, Susan, and Meredith Michaels. *The Mommy Myth: The Idealization of Motherhood and How It Has Undermined Women*. New York: Free Press, 2004.

Elias, Maurice, Steven E. Tobias, and Brian S. Friedlander. *Emotionally Intelligent Parenting: How to Raise a Self-Disciplined, Responsible, Socially Skilled Child*. New York: Three Rivers Press, 1999.

Fox, Annie. *Teen Survival Guide to Dating and Relating: Real-World Advice on Guys, Girls, Growing Up, and Getting Along*. Minneapolis: Free Spirit, 2005.

Gerber, Robin. *Leadership the Eleanor Roosevelt Way: Timeless Strategies from the First Lady of Courage*. Upper Saddle River, N.J.: Prentice Hall, 2002.

Heifetz, Ronald A., and Donald L. Laurie. "The Work of Leadership." *Harvard Business Review*, Dec. 2001, pp. 4–14.

Hochschild, Arlie R. *The Second Shift*. New York: Penguin Books, 1989, 2003.

Hochschild, Arlie R. *The Time Bind: When Work Becomes Home and Home Becomes Work*. New York: Henry Holt, 1997.

Kohn, Alfie. *Unconditional Parenting: A Provocative Challenge to the Conventional Wisdom About Discipline*. New York: Atria Books, 2005.

Kouzes, James M., and Barry Z. Posner. *The Leadership Challenge*. San Francisco: Jossey-Bass, 2002.

Kouzes, James M., and Barry Z. Posner. *Credibility: How Leaders Gain and Lose It, Why People Demand It*. San Francisco: Jossey-Bass, 2003.

Kouzes, James M., and Barry, Z. Posner. *Encouraging the Heart*. San Francisco: Jossey-Bass, 2003.

Lerner, Richard, and Laurence, Steinberg. (Eds.). *The Handbook of Adolescent Psychology*. Hoboken, N.J.: Wiley, 2004.

Levine, Madeline. *The Price of Privilege: How Parental Pressure and Material Advantage Are Creating a Generation of Disconnected and Unhappy Kids*. New York: HarperCollins, 2006.

Lezin, Nicole, Lori A. Rolleri, Steve Bean, and Julie Taylor. *Parent-Child Connectedness: Implications for Research, Interventions, and Positive Impacts on Adolescent Health*. New York: ETR Associates, 2004.

Libbey, Heather. "Measuring Student Relationships to School: Attachment, Bonding and Connectedness." *Journal of School Health*, 2004, 74(7), 274.

Maddi, Salvatore R., and Deborah M. Khoshaba. *Resilience at Work: How to Succeed No Matter What Life Throws at You.* New York: AMACOM, 2005.

Mogel, Wendy. *The Blessing of a Skinned Knee.* New York: Penguin Books, 2001.

Ochs, Lisa E., and Elinor Capps. *Living Narrative: Creating Lives in Everyday Storytelling.* Boston: Harvard University Press, 2001.

Quinn, Robert E. "Moments of Greatness: Entering the Fundamental State of Leadership." *Harvard Business Review,* Aug. 2005, pp. 1–9.

Riera, Michael. *Uncommon Sense for Parents with Teenagers.* Berkeley, Calif.: Celestial Arts, 1995.

Rosener, Judy B. "Ways Women Lead." *Harvard Business Review,* Dec. 1990, pp. 3–10.

Schein, Edgar H. *Organizational Culture and Leadership.* San Francisco: Jossey-Bass, 1992.

Segal, Julius. *Winning Life's Toughest Battles: Roots of Human Resilience.* New York: Ballantine, 1987.

Sherman, Michael. "Family Narratives: Internal Representations of Family Relationships and Affective Themes." *Infant Mental Health Journal,* 1990, *11*(3), 253–258.

Siegel, Daniel J., and Mary Hartzell. *Parenting from the Inside Out: How a Deeper Self-Understanding Can Help You Raise Children Who Thrive.* New York: Penguin Group, 2003.

Stone, Douglas, Bruce Patton, and Sheila Heen. *Difficult Conversations: How to Discuss What Matters Most.* New York: Penguin Books, 1999.

Wolf, Anthony E. *Get out of My Life, but First Could You Drive Me and Cheryl to the Mall: A Parent's Guide to the New Teenager.* (Rev. ed.) New York: Farrar, Straus and Giroux, 2002.

# ABOUT THE AUTHOR

Jamie Woolf has over twenty years of experience consulting to business leaders. Distilling what she has learned through her work inside dozens of organizations, Jamie lays out her "best practices" in this book to help parents enjoy more success at home and at work. She authors a blog at www.mominchief.com. She founded The Parent Leader to help mothers and fathers gain the self-awareness and leadership skills to transform their daily parenting challenges into desired results; she also cofounded Pinehurst Consulting, an organization development and training consulting firm. She serves on the advisory board of Working Mother Media.

Jamie holds an M.S. in industrial/organizational psychology from San Francisco State University, and a B.A. in psychology from the University of California, Santa Cruz. She lives in Oakland, California, with her husband and two daughters.

# INDEX